INTRODUCING

Feminism

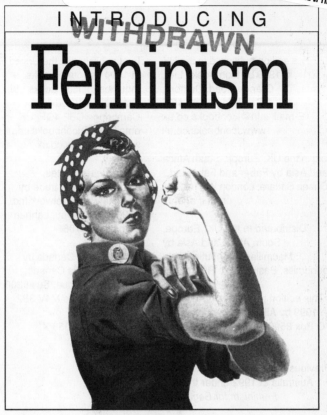

Susan Alice Watkins, Marisa Rueda & Marta Rodriguez

Edited by Richard Appignanesi

ICON BOOKS UK   TOTEM BOOKS USA

This edition published in the UK
in 1999 by Icon Books Ltd.,
Grange Road, Duxford,
Cambridge CB2 4QF
E-mail: info@iconbooks.co.uk
www.iconbooks.co.uk

Sold in the UK, Europe, South Africa
and Asia by Faber and Faber Ltd.,
3 Queen Square, London WC1N 3AU
or their agents

Distributed in the UK, Europe,
South Africa and Asia by
Macmillan Distribution Ltd.,
Houndmills, Basingstoke RG21 6XS

This edition published in Australia
in 1999 by Allen & Unwin Pty. Ltd.,
PO Box 8500, 83 Alexander Street,
Crows Nest, NSW 2065

Previously published in the UK and
Australia in 1992 under the title
Feminism for Beginners

Reprinted 1993, 1995, 1997, 1999, 2001

First published in the United States
in 1994 by Totem Books
Inquiries to: Icon Books Ltd.,
Grange Road, Duxford,
Cambridge CB2 4QF, UK
email: info@iconbooks.co.uk
www.iconbooks.co.uk

In the United States,
distributed to the trade by
National Book Network Inc.,
4720 Boston Way, Lanham,
Maryland 20706

Distributed in Canada by
Penguin Books Canada,
10 Alcorn Avenue, Suite 300,
Toronto, Ontario M4V 3B2

ISBN 1 84046 058 X

Originating editor: Richard Appignanesi

Printed and bound in Australia
by McPherson's Printing Group, Victoria

What is feminism?

Women demanding their full rights as human beings!

CHALLENGING THE RELATIONS BETWEEN MEN (AS A GROUP) AND WOMEN (AS ANOTHER)...

...AND REBELLING AGAINST ALL POWER STRUCTURES, LAWS AND CONVENTIONS THAT KEEP WOMEN SERVILE, SUBORDINATE AND SECOND BEST.

WOMEN CONSCIOUSLY WORKING TOGETHER FOR OUR RIGHTS - THAT'S THE ONLY WAY WE'LL WIN THEM!

Feminism is about challenging the division of labour in the world that puts men in charge of the public sphere - work, sports, wars, government - while women slave away unpaid in the home, carrying the whole burden of family life.

Before the Dawn of Feminism

History provides many individual examples of women who possessed extraordinary power, courage and talent. Such women are known to us as famous empresses and queens, brave women warriors, saints, witches, scientists, poets and artists. They are the celebrities of women's history. But they stand out as individual exceptions who did not (and could not) significantly affect or improve the status of the vast majority of ordinary, oppressed women.

Boadicea (died Warrior Queen wh defied the Roman Conquerors Bru

Lady Murasaki Shikibu (c. 978-1026) Japanese. Author of the first full length novel The Tale of Genji.

Queen Elizabeth I (1533-1603). Britain's great sovereign who inspired the English Renaissance.

The story of changing the subordinate condition of women begins with feminism. And when does feminism begin? The answer is, when women begin consciously to organize themselves on a scale large enough and effective enough to improve their situation. But that took many many centuries. For a very long time, the odds were hopelessly stacked against any possibility of organized feminist action.

Sor Juana Inés de la Cruz
1651- -1695

Sister Juana Inés, Mexican scholar and poet, can serve as a model of the "independent woman" in the centuries before emancipation. She made a choice, typical of her time - the convent instead of marriage, husband and children. Inside the cloister, she had time at least to study and write the first masterpieces of Latin American poetry. Even so, the Inquisition finally silenced her.

The injustices suffered by women in the name of romance, caused Sor Juana no less indignation than the lack of educational opportunities. The infamous double-standard that has historically plagued male-female relationships did not escape her notice and she described it with deadly accuracy:

Accusing women wrongly,
you are very foolish men,
if you do not see you cause
the very thing you condemn.

If with unmatched anxiety
you solicit their disdain,
why demand their virtue,
while encouraging to sin?

You combat her resistance
and then, gravely you recount,
it was woman's wanton ways
that brought you to this point.

Who bears the greater blame,
in this passion that's a loser?
she who's fallen to his lure
or he, who, fallen, lures her?

Or who's the guilty one,
though rightly neither's free from stain
she who's sinning for her pay,
or he who's paying for the sin?

The Feudal Past...

Until the 18th century, European societies were restricted to a feudal system of kings, big landowning nobles and clerics ruling over small-scale artisans, merchants and peasants. Work was mostly done close to home, on the farm or in the workshop. Although their tasks and pay were different, men and women worked together.

But then the spread of manufacturing industries and bigger cities began separating work from home, men's work from women's, and creating for the first time the idea of the male "breadwinner" and the economically dependent "housewife".

FEUDALISM GAVE US A CERTAIN SECURITY...

...BUT IT WAS A BIT UNNATURAL!

...and Natural Rights

The growth of industrialization gave birth to new social classes - the landless labourer and the rising urban middle-class.

New insecurities create a new thirst for freedom!

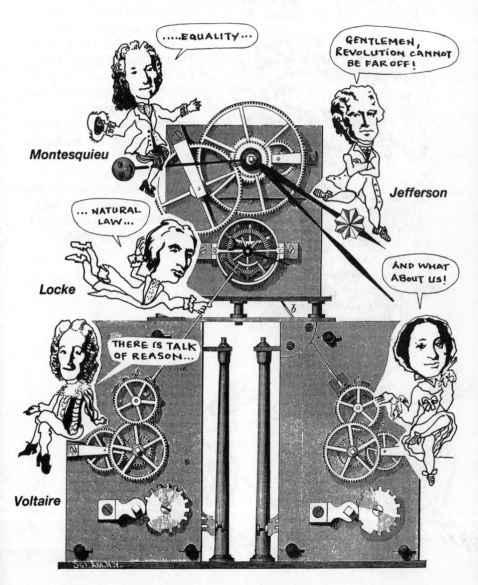

The Age of Enlightenment

By the mid-18th century, an international group of enlightened thinkers had begun to challenge the tyranny of feudal societies based on the inherited privileges of kings, Church and nobles. Against the "Divine Right" of kings, these enlightened critics opposed the "Rights of Man". They vocalized the dissatisfactions of a new and growing middle-class, eager for progress and fed up with the inequalities of an old, rigid and corrupt feudal hierarchy.

Amid this ferment, women began to raise the question of **their** inequality - and to challenge the domestic tyranny of MEN!

One of the chief enlightenment philosophers was Jean-Jaques Rousseau (1712-78), a watch-maker's son from Geneva. He attacked all the social injustices - but typically he overlooked one. In **Emile** (1762), his seminal work on education, this is what Rousseau wrote...

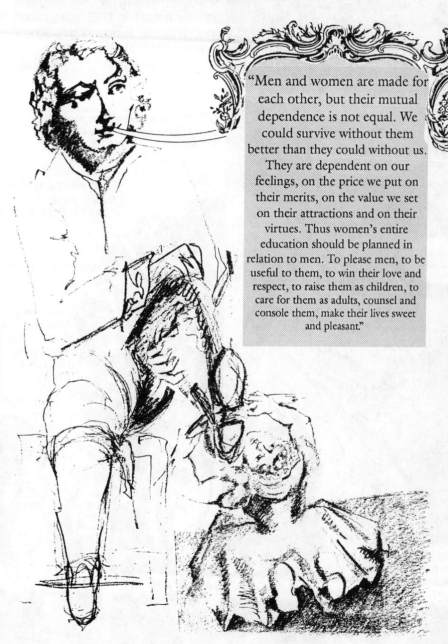

"Men and women are made for each other, but their mutual dependence is not equal. We could survive without them better than they could without us. They are dependent on our feelings, on the price we put on their merits, on the value we set on their attractions and on their virtues. Thus women's entire education should be planned in relation to men. To please men, to be useful to them, to win their love and respect, to raise them as children, to care for them as adults, counsel and console them, make their lives sweet and pleasant."

Mary, Mary, quite contrary...

Meanwhile, across the Channel in England, a strong-willed and rebellious little girl was growing up who would challenge these self-satisfied masculine pieties. *Mary Wollstonecraft* (1759- 97) was born into a farming family dominated by a noisy, shiftless father prone to fits of drunken violence, and an easy-going, Irish-born mother.

Mary was determined to enjoy a full and active life. She knew from bitter personal experience of the obstacles facing an independent woman struggling to earn her own living and educate herself. In 1783, Mary raised enough money to open a girls school in Newington Green, a north London suburb.

OH! NOT ANOTHER DAUGHTER!

I PREFER MY SON!

WHAT WAS CALLED SPIRIT AND WIT IN HIM, WAS CRUELLY REPRESSED IN ME.

THE STAFF CONSISTED OF MY SISTERS, MY FRIEND FANNY BLOOD AND MYSELF.

WE NEVER HAD MORE THAN A DOZEN PUPILS.

AND WE WERE NOVICE TEACHERS, TRYING TO EDUCATE OURSELVES TOO!

Mary's neighbours were Dissenters - radical Presbyterians, Baptists and Independents banned from all civil or municipal government posts and from the universities. They formed their own Dissenting Academies where freedom of debate prevailed and Age of Enlightenment ideas were openly discussed.

In 1786, Mary suffered a number of misfortunes - the death of her friend, Fanny, the bankruptcy of her school, and a year as governess to the aristocratic Kingsboroughs in Ireland.

LEGITIMATE POLITICAL POWER RESTS WITH THE CONSENT OF THE PEOPLE.

NOT WITH KINGS OR ARISTOCRATIC PRIVILEGE.

FIVE HOURS TO DRESS DOES NOT SEEM EXCESSIVE TO ME.

AS CITIZENS OF THE WORLD IT IS OUR DUTY TO SUPPORT THE AMERICAN REVOLUTION!

Lady Kingsborough is as indifferent to the education of her children as she is to the wretchedness of the peasants on whom her idleness and dissipation depends.

13

Mary's dissenting friends put her in touch with Joseph Johnson, a London publisher who championed the cause of all the oppressed - slaves, Jews, chimney-sweeps, abused animals, the homeless and hungry. Mary became a central member of Johnson's circle in 1788, meeting regularly with other radical writers in his printing house in St. Paul's Churchyard.

In 1789, the French Revolution erupted. The political temperature in England rose to fever pitch in response.

William Blake

Joseph Johnson

William Wordsworth

Mary Hayes

William Goodwin

Tom Paine

Mary Wollstonecraft

The Royal Tyranny of Kings &
the Domestic Tyranny of Men

Mary's friend, Tom Paine, had returned to England after 15 years in America where he had experienced the bracing revolutionary climate of constitutional experiment. Tom Paine defended the American and French constitutionalists in his highly influential book, **The Rights of Man** (1791-92).
Paine's book earned him a death sentence for treason against the British Crown in 1792. He escaped to France, thanks to Blake's timely warning.

Mary sat down to write her own famous 300-page appeal, **A Vindication of the Rights of Woman** (1792), in which for the first time Enlightenment ideas were applied to the situation of women. It was an instant best-seller and the foundation stone of modern feminism.

Mary had put her finger exactly on the chief obstacle that had prevented women from taking action to achieve equality - **domestic tyranny!** Denial of political rights, education and equal work for women was tyranny. And a woman's financial dependence on a man in marriage was "legal prostitution".

For the vast majority of women, they are still a long way off. Mary argued that femininity was a **construct** - women are born equal but taught to be subordinate, weak and feather-headed. "She is brought up to be the toy of a man, his rattle and must jingle in his ears whenever, dismissing reason he chooses to be amused."

Mary's clarion call in **A Vindication of the Rights of Woman** (1792) has rung down the centuries. Her demands for an end to the double standards of male and female behaviour, for women's rights to independent work, education, civil and political life still form the basis of feminism today.

She deplored the division of labour between breadwinning husbands and their wives kept at home, "confined in cages, like the feathered race. It is true that they are provided with food and raiment, for which they neither toil nor spin; but health, liberty and virtue are given in exchange".

She called for universal co-education and women's right to work in the trades and professions: "Women may study the art of healing and be physicians as well as nurses.

I do earnestly wish to see the distinction of sex abolished altogether ... save where love is concerned!

They might also study politics and businesses of all kinds, if they were educated in a more orderly manner. How many women thus waste life away, who might have practised as physician, regulated a farm, managed a shop, and stood erect supported by their own industry, instead of hanging their heads?"

She went as far as to suggest that women should have their own political representatives, instead of being arbitrarily governed by men.

I DO NOT WANT TO BE LOVED AS A GODDESS, BUT I WANT TO BE NECESSARY TO YOU...

In 1793, Mary went to Paris to see the Revolution for herself. And there, aged 34, she fell deeply in love with an American ex-army captain, Gilbert Imlay (1754-1828). Mary's hopes for a lifelong relationship did not suit Imlay, an adventurer involved in shady business dealings.

Mary was left pregnant and alone at the height of the Terror when countless victims lost their heads to the guillotine. She poured out a torrent of letters to Imlay. "My soul is weary - I'm sick at heart." He joined her briefly when their baby, Fanny, was born, but soon sent her on a 6-month money-raising expedition to Scandinavia while he set up home with an actress.

In 1795, worn out by the love affair, Mary attempted suicide by jumping off Putney Bridge. She failed to drown herself but it cured her of Imlay. Alas, she had only two more years to live.

Mary again set about earning a living for herself. She began a relationship with the anarchist philosopher William Godwin who had stood up for the English republicans during the treason trials of the 1790s. She died in 1797 giving birth to a daughter, another Mary, who grew up to marry the Romantic poet Percy Bysshe Shelley and to create one of the finest works of science-fiction ever written, **Frankenstein** (1818).

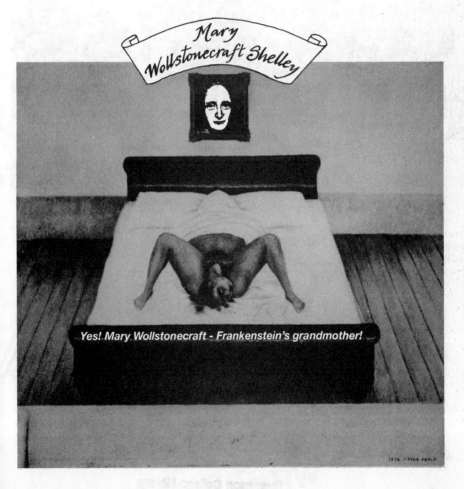

Yes! Mary Wollstonecraft - Frankenstein's grandmother!

The French Revolution: 1789

Mary Wollstonecraft was not alone. The French Revolution offered women a chance to do away with the old conditions on a social level, not just an individual one.

The working women of Paris were the first to take matters into their own hands. In October 1789, while the gentlemen of the Constituent Assembly busied themselves with their debates about the new French Constitution, the *sans-culottes* women - laundry-women, seamstresses, servants, shop-girls, workers' wives - were complaining about the scarcity of food. Some 6,000 women marched on the Town Hall of Paris demanding cheaper bread.

They were angry, and they weren't prepared to take NO for an answer.

Jacobin Women

Revolutionaries in France were split between the radical Jacobins who wanted to do away with the Monarchy and the moderate Girondins who wanted a Constitutional Monarchy.

One group in Paris that sympathized with the Jacobins was the **Citoyennes Républicaines Révolutionnaires** (Revolutionary Republican Women Citizens). They wore a uniform of red and white striped pantaloons and red "liberty bonnets" and carried arms in their demonstrations. They called for women's right to vote and to hold the highest civilian and military posts in the new Republic.

Girondin Women

It was under the Girondins that the Assembly passed a pro-women divorce law. Many early feminists perished with the Girondin party during the Jacobin Terror of 1793.

Olympe de Gouge (1748-93) was a Girondin, born Marie Gouze, the illegitimate daughter of a nobleman and a butcher's wife from Montauban in the south of France. She rebelled against the narrow prejudices of her home town and the way her father had treated her mother. Marriage and two children confirmed her disillusionment. She ran away to Paris, changed her name and went on stage.

Soon she was writing plays and pamphlets too, calling for the abolition of the slave trade, public workshops for the unemployed and a national theatre for women.

In 1791, Olympe published the **Declaration of the Rights of Women,** in answer to the Assembly's Declaration of the Rights of Man, calling for equal rights in law, government and education.

Women awake!

The tocsin of reason is being heard throughout the whole universe: discover your rights!

The powerful empire of nature is no longer surrounded by prejudice, fanaticism, superstition and lies.

Courageously oppose the force of reason to the empty pretensions of superiority, unite yourselves.

Oh women,

Deploy all the energy of your character and you will soon see these haughty men. Not grovelling at your feet as servile adorers but proud to share the treasures of the Supreme Being!

Olympe was too much of a troublemaker to survive the Jacobin Terror. Although a Republican, she published an appeal against the King's execution. It cost Olympe her head.

Scaffolds and executioners - are these then the results of the Revolution that should have been the glory of France, spreading without distinction over the two sexes and serving as a model to the universe? -she cried as she was led to her death.

Théroigne de Méricourt (1766-1817) was another outspoken critic of the male-dominated course of the Revolution. She was born Anne-Josephe Terwagne, the daughter of a poor farming couple in the Ardennes.
She came to Paris and made a living as a courtesan before the Revolution.

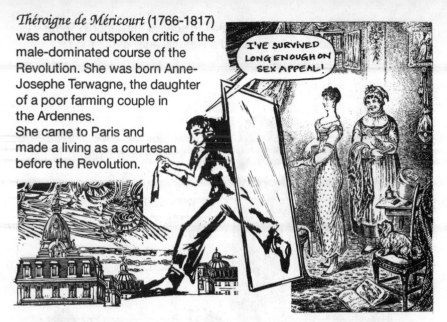

I'VE SURVIVED LONG ENOUGH ON SEX APPEAL!

Soon she was making speeches to large, open-air women's meetings, dressed in riding-clothes to give herself greater freedom of movement.

IT IS TIME AT LAST THAT WOMEN SHOULD THROW ASIDE THEIR SHAMEFUL INACTIVITY IN WHICH IGNORANCE, PRIDE AND THE INJUSTICE OF MEN HAVE KEPT THEM FOR SO LONG. LET US RETURN TO THE TIMES WHEN OUR MOTHERS, THE GAULS AND PROUD GERMANS, SPOKE IN THE PUBLIC ASSEMBLIES, AND FOUGHT BESIDE THEIR HUSBANDS.

SHE'S JUST A GIRONDIN WHORE IN BREECHES!

SHE VIOLATES NATURE ITSELF! A WOMAN'S PLACE IS AT HOME.

Théroigne also allied herself with the Girondins. She was far too conspicuous to avoid being victimized. In June 1793, she was attacked by a band of Jacobin women as she walked through the Tuileries gardens.

STRIP HER NAKED!

STONE HER!

STRIP HER NAKED!

DEATH TO THE KING AND ALL GIRONDIN TRAITORS!

The stoning damaged poor Théroigne's brain, and she never recovered.

She suffered from headaches and persistent "melancholy". She was confined in the Salpêtrière lunatic asylum for the rest of her life. French feminism languished with her.

AFRO-AMERICAN PIONEERS

In the United States, a different sort of pattern emerged in the fight for women's rights. If the struggles for democratic freedoms in the French Revolution had first given European women a glimpse of the possibility of overthrowing "the domestic tyranny of men", in the United States it was the movement against slavery that gave women, black and white, the opportunity to organize politically against their own oppression.

ANYWAY, SLAVE MARRIAGES ARE ILLEGAL BUT RAPE ISN'T!

WHITE WOMEN ARE VIRTUALLY PRISONERS OF THEIR FAMILIES.

AH, BUT BLACK WOMEN ARE VIOLENTLY TORN AWAY FROM THEIRS.

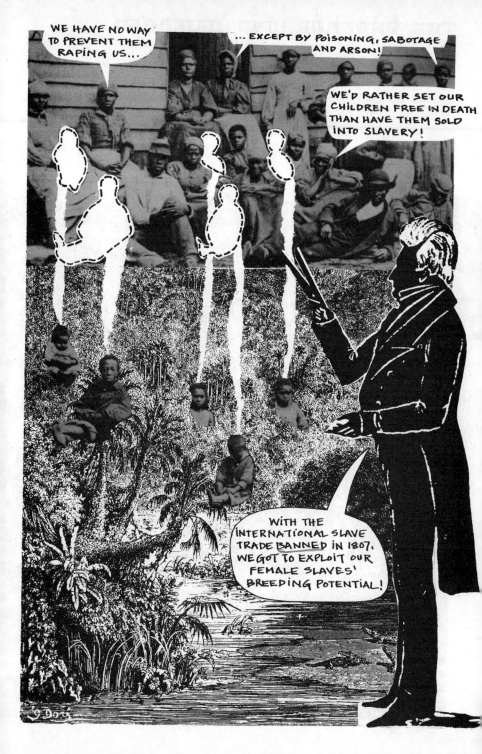

29

THE UNDERGROUND RAILROAD

Other black women risked their lives on the "Underground Railroad", an undercover escape route to the North from the Southern slave states. *Harriet Tubman* (1823-1913) was a slave born in Maryland. She was a tough, adventurous little girl. Harriet ran away with her brothers when she was 25.

It's too risky, Harriet.

We are going back... Well, I'm going o

THERE WAS ONE OF TWO THINGS I HAD THE RIGHT TO – LIBERTY OR DEATH.

Harriet Tubman

Harriet became one of the most famous "conductors" on the Railroad, bringing over 300 slaves to freedom through unimaginable risks. Most of the runaways were young men, but Harriet brought out women with babies and little children too.

Ellen Craft (1826-91) was born in Clinton, Georgia, to a plantation owner, John Smith, who already had half-a-dozen white children with his wife and as many mixed race ones. He raped Helen's mother, a house slave, when she was 17.

In her twenties, Ellen managed to move out of the house into a one-room cabin of her own, earning her living by dress-making. She fell in love with a local cabinet-maker, William Craft. Their owners gave them permission to live together.

Ellen cropped her hair and disguised herself as a white Southern gentleman on his way North for medical treatment, her arm in a sling as an excuse to avoid writing.

The terrifying journey by train and steamship lasted over a week, with Ellen surrounded by hard-drinking plantation owners.

Ellen and William set up home in the free black quarter of Boston. They became major speakers in the Anti-Slavery Society until the 1850 Fugitive Slave Law forced them to flee again, this time to England. After the Civil War, they returned to Georgia and bought a run-down plantation where Ellen ran a school for black children for many years, until she died.

Sojourner Truth (1797-1883) was born Isabella to second-generation slaves working for a Dutch-speaking landowner in Ulster County, New York.

In 1827, she fled with her youngest child, Sophia, and managed to free her son Peter from an Alabama slave-owner to whom he had been illegally sold. With them, she went to New York and got work as a maid.

She joined some New York evangelists working the notorious "Five Points" red-light district and became a member of the African Zion Church.

In 1843, her children grown, *"she set out walking, singing and preaching, sleeping wherever I could"*.

In Massachusetts, she encountered the Abolitionists and through them, the new women's rights movement. Sojourner could silence any man who dared say women were "too frail for public life".

"AND AIN'T I A WOMAN?"

In 1833, *Sarah Mapp Douglass* (1806-82), a young black Quaker schoolteacher from Philadelphia, set up the Female Anti-Slavery Society with *Harriet Purvis, Sarah* and *Margaretta Forten* and some white Quaker women, among them *Lucretia Mott*.

It was from the courage and the tenacity of these Afro-American women and from the platforms of the Anti-Slavery Society that the white pioneers of the American women's rights movement drew their original inspiration and political education.

WILL YOU JOIN US, SISTER LUCRETIA?

Frederick Douglass

LIBERTY LINE.
NEW ARRANGEMENT---NIGHT AND DAY.

STRUGGLE FOR WOMEN'S RIGHTS

"I AM A QUAKER BROUGHT UP TO SPEAK AND PREACH IN PUBLIC. YES, I'LL SPEAK FOR YOUR ANTI-SLAVERY SOCIETY! WHO KNOWS BUT THAT IF WOMAN ACTED HER PART IN GOVERNMENTAL AFFAIRS, THERE MIGHT BE AN ENTIRE CHANGE IN THE TURMOIL OF POLITICAL LIFE?"

Lucretia Mott (1793-1850) combined a fiery determination with a hatred of injustice and a strong sense of the ridiculous. She was a sea captain's daughter, born and raised on the island of Nantucket among strong, independent women whose husbands were often away at sea for years.

Lucretia always kept a copy of Mary Wollstonecraft's **Vindication of the Rights of Women** on her living room table.

Tirelessly, Lucretia combined preaching and school-teaching with raising five children.

On the question of slavery that was then dividing the Quaker movement from top to bottom, she took a strong and principled stand, dragging her husband along behind her.

When the family moved to Philadelphia, Lucretia was quickly drawn into the thick of the Anti-Slavery Society and took a firm stand on the disputes that were rocking it.

SHOULD BLACKS BE ALLOWED TO PARTICIPATE EQUALLY WITH WHITES?

YES, YES, WITHOUT A QUESTION! WHY SHOULD WOMAN NOT SEEK TO BE A REFORMER? TRULY IT IS A MOURNFUL PROSPECT FOR WOMAN IF SHE IS TO BE SATISFIED WITH THE NARROW SPHERE ASSIGNED HER BY MAN!

SHOULD WOMEN BE ALLOWED TO SPEAK OUT AT PUBLIC MEETINGS?

Racist mobs, whipped up by the white mayor of Philadelphia, attacked the hall when Lucretia chaired her first meeting of the Female Anti-Slavery Society in 1833. Two sisters who were speaking at the meeting, *Sarah* (1792-1873) and *Angelina Grimke* (1805-79) particularly attracted the wrath of the crowd.

MAN HAS SUBJECTED WOMAN TO HIS WILL AND USED HER FOR HIS OWN SELFISHNESS AND COMFORT. HE HAS DONE EVERYTHING HE COULD TO DEBASE AND ENSLAVE HER MIND.

...AND NOW HE LOOKS TRIUMPHANTLY ON THE RUIN WHICH HE HAS WROUGHT AND SAYS THAT SHE IS INFERIOR!

They were the daughters of a rich, white Charleston plantation-owner and had broken with the traditions of their family, race, class and sex to come and denounce slavery before a mixed audience.

Despite continuing opposition, the anti-slavery women's determination to be heard was beginning to win space for them within the Anti-Slavery Society. Not so in England, where Lucretia and James attended the International Anti-Slavery Convention in 1840, along with a young bride Elizabeth Cady Stanton and her husband Henry who were on their honeymoon. The Convention ground to a halt as a furious battle was waged behind the scenes - should the female delegates from the U.S. be permitted to take part?

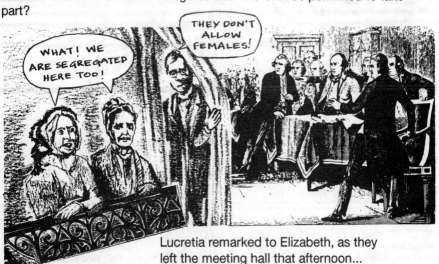

Lucretia remarked to Elizabeth, as they left the meeting hall that afternoon...

Elizabeth Cady Stanton (1815-1902) was a prosperous judge's daughter from Albany, New York. The judge's only son died in childhood, and Elizabeth strove to take his place in her father's eyes by achieving brilliant results at school. It was no use...

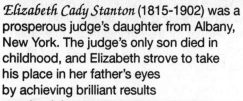

I WAS TOLD – "YOU WON'T BE ALLOWED TO ENTER WITH THE BOYS IN YOUR CLASS". I FELT SHATTERED!

Meanwhile, her father's law students lost no chance to belittle the independent girl. When she showed one of them her Christmas gifts, a necklace and bracelet, these became a lesson on "property rights"!

If you were my wife, these would be mine, and you'd wear them only with my permission. I could even exchange them for a cigar and you could watch them evaporate in smoke!

Elizabeth rebelled against her conservative family by marrying an Abolitionist. But the real turning point in her life was her meeting with Lucretia Mott. Together they decided to launch a movement for the emancipation of women - although, after her marriage, she found herself drowning in domesticity in the isolated little rural town of Seneca Falls, New York.

I AM ABOUT TO DIE OF INTELLECTUAL REPRESSION!

NEVER MIND THAT! WE'VE ONLY GOT FOUR DAYS TO DRAFT OUR PROPOSALS FOR THE WOMEN'S RIGHTS CONVENTION.

And so the **Seneca Falls Declaration of Sentiments** was drawn up around the parlour table:

We hold these truths to be self-evident: that all men and women are created equal...
The history of mankind is a history of repeated injuries and usurpations on the part of man toward woman, having in direct object the establishment of an absolute tyranny over her...
He has never permitted her to exercise her inalienable right to the effective franchise...
He has made her, if married, in the eyes of the law, civilly dead...

THE FIRST WOMEN'S RIGHTS CONVENTION

One hundred men and women packed into the little Wesleyan chapel at Seneca Falls, 10 a.m. on the 19th July 1848. With beating heart, Elizabeth rose to propose a resolution so radical that even Lucretia would not support it...

After much argument, Elizabeth's motion was passed by the narrowest majority. The meeting was attacked in nearly every East Coast newspaper - and Elizabeth Cady Stanton was famous overnight. Women's rights campaigners flocked to her house in Seneca Falls - among them, the woman who became Elizabeth's best friend and ally: *Susan B. Anthony.*

Susan B. Anthony (1820-1906) was single, with a stern, Evangelical streak, the very opposite of pleasure-loving Elizabeth. Her father had owned a cotton mill in Battenville, N.Y., before going bust in the crash of 1837.

Susan left school scarred by her experiences. Her lifelong friendship with Elizabeth gave her the love to heal her childhood wounds and the encouragement to fight for a better world for women.

Throughout the 1850s and 60s, Susan was the organizer, arranging meetings, booking halls, printing handbills, tracts and posters. Elizabeth, surrounded by 8 children, wrote the speeches.

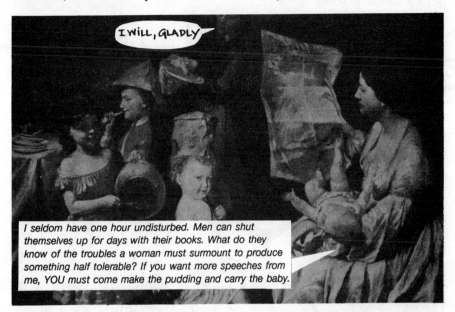

Seneca Falls became Susan's second home. Elizabeth's husband Henry was a successful politician often absent for long periods at the State legislature. The two women shared the childcare and the housekeeping, snatching moments to read and write. But when evening came...Peace!

From their dreams and hard work came the inspiration for the entire U.S. women's rights movement of the last century.

Elizabeth and Susan spoke at endless meetings up and down the country. They campaigned for improved conditions for women schoolteachers, for married women's rights to their own wages and property, to education, careers, and votes.

It was hard work....

...travelling to speak at tiny meetings, often facing hostility and abuse.

Elizabeth appealed to the New York State legislature against the law that compelled an employer to pay a woman's wages to her husband Susan spent 5 months gathering signatures for this petition. Progress was slow and often disheartening... but worthwhile.

By the mid-1850s, State legislatures began showing sympathy towards women's property rights. By 1860, some 14 States had passed reforms.

Lucy Stone (1818-83) was another visitor to Seneca Falls. Plain and thin, weighing less than 45 kilos, she was raised in poverty on a small Massachusetts farm.

She was determined to escape her mother's fate and get herself to college.

Working day and night teaching in the village school for $1 a week as well as labouring on the farm, Lucy was 25 before she saved enough money to pay her fare and a half-year's tuition on the "ladies' course" at Oberlin College, Ohio.

Oberlin was the only co-ed, mixed race college in the country. For Lucy, it was a revelation. Many of the black students had come from the South on the Underground Railroad. Others, like Lucy, had to work full-time to pay their way.

Antoinette Brown (1825-1921) became the first woman to be ordained in the US.

50

Lucy became a gifted speaker for Abolitionism and women's rights. At open air meetings all over Massachusetts, she often faced a hail of hymnbooks, stones and rotten fruit.

I remember the time Lucy got the better of a mob by addressing a ruffian who was about to hit her with his stick, and she said ...

THIS MAN WILL TAKE CARE OF ME!

The ruffian was too astonished for words when Lucy took his arm. He became her protector, preserving order with his raised club until Lucy finished her speech.

Lucy married the dashing young Abolitionist, Henry Blackwell, when she was 37. Antoinette married his brother Samuel and had 7 children. Motherhood put the brakes on Lucy's activities.

"I went to a lecture on Joan of Arc this evening. It was very inspiring, and for an hour I felt all things were possible. But when I came home and looked in Alice's sleeping face... I saw that for these years I can only be a mother."

Didn't I warn you against Domestic Tyranny?

Susan B. Anthony was the only pioneering women's rights agitator to steer clear of what she ironically called "the ineffable joys of maternity". She complained to Antoinette when Lucy showed up unprepared at an important State legislature meeting after Alice had been ill.

The early pioneers split after the storms of the Civil War (1860-65). Lucy and Antoinette supported the 15th Amendment that gave black males the vote. Susan and Elizabeth opposed it on the grounds that it denied the vote to women. Two different women's suffrage organizations were set up that went on campaigning separately.

In 1888, they all came together again, 40 years after Seneca Falls, to form the united National American Woman's Suffrage Association. Lucy's daughter, Alice Stone Blackwell, was a moving spirit of the new Association.

Lucy whispered her dying words to Alice...

BRITISH WOMEN'S MOVEMENT: 1850-1914

Work...

By the mid-19th century, the Industrial Revolution and the wealth of the British Empire had created an army of working women - mill-girls, domestic servants and farm labourers, milliners, seamstresses and governesses. Of these, the most independent were the factory workers in the new mill-towns of Lancashire and Yorkshire.

In previous centuries, women had usually worked at home under their fathers or husbands, on the farm or in a craft workshop or domestic industry. In the new factories, the girls worked crowded together, free from parental restraints - and for the first time got their wages in hand each week. Factory girls were in a minority. Most working women at the time were domestic servants, policed by their employers. Their hours were longer and their pay far lower than factory workers.

...or Marriage

All women's work was insecure, irregular and worse paid than men's. Women were rigidly excluded from the professions and education. Economically and socially, a woman's best hope of providing for herself lay in marriage.

The role expected of the middle-class Victorian wife was very different from that of the farmer's or artisan's wife in previous centuries when production was based round the home. She had no place in the world.

Married women were not so much "angels in the home" as prisoners there. Single women at least had the right to own their own earnings and property. Upon marriage, they forfeited that. All a wife's income henceforth became her husband's - and she could end up like Mrs. Rochester in Charlotte Bronte's novel **Jane Eyre** (1847), "the mad woman in the attic".

In practice many middle-class men delayed marriage until they were in their forties.

By the mid-19th century, there was a "surplus" of single middle-class women, denied proper education, work (beyond governessing) and their rights as citizens. Although better off than working-class women, it was clear to middle-class ones that their economic chains were forged on the ideological anvil of men's superiority. But it would take **three generations** of British feminists to win the most basic civil rights for women - the right to an education, to keep their own earnings and to vote.

First Generation: The Ladies of Langham Place

Barbara Leigh Smith (later *Mrs. Bodichon*) (1827-91) was born into a large, lively and unorthodox family. Her father was the radical Member of Parliament, Benjamin Leigh Smith. Her mother, Anne Longdon, a milliner, died when Barbara was seven. The two were never married, so the family was taboo to their stuffier relations. The Leigh Smith household was a centre for abolitionists, political refugees and activists. Barbara's close friend Bessie first remembered him kneeling down to tie his daughter's shoelaces...

Barbara scandalized the villagers with her blue-tinted spectacles - and we didn't wear corsets!

Barbara's teen-age friend *Bessie Rayner Parkes* (1829-1925) also came from a radical family. In 1850, they set off unchaperoned on a grand sketching tour of Europe.

WE WERE SHOCKED BY THE DESPOTISM IN GERMANY AND AUSTRIA AFTER THE VIOLENT CRUSHING OF THE 1848 REVOLUTIONS.

The Pre-Raphaelite artist Dante Gabriel Rossetti (1828-82) said to his sister the poet Christina Rossetti (1830-94):

Blessed with large rations of cash, fat, enthusiasm and golden hair, Barbara thinks nothing of climbing up a mountain in breeches, or wading through a stream in none.

19 Langham Place

In 1856, Barbara and Bessie organized a committee to collect petitions for a Married Woman's Property Bill (a wife's right to keep her own property and income). In 1858, they launched the **Englishwoman's Journal** to debate issues of women's work, education, legal rights and the vote. In 1859, they founded the Society for Promoting the Employment of Women which set up a women's printshop, the Victoria Press, run by Emily Faithfull and her task force of women compositors. There was also a Ladies' Institute at **19 Langham Place**. Dr. Elizabeth Blackwell, the first woman doctor in the US, was a speaker at Langham Place.

...EVEN IF IT MEANT DISSECTING CADAVERS IN MY BEDROOM WHEN I WAS DENIED ACCESS TO THE DISSECTING ROOMS!

Elizabeth Garrett

I ENCOURAGED ELIZABETH GARRETT (1836-1917) TO BREAK INTO THE BRITISH MEDICAL PROFESSION...

Elizabeth Blackwell

Emily Davies (1830-1921) was a founder of Girton College Cambridge in 1873. Others were Elizabeth Gaskell, Elizabeth Barrett Browning, George Eliot, Anna Jameson.

In 1865, the "Ladies of Langham Place" organized petitions for a Women's Suffrage Bill to be presented to Parliament by a newly-elected Member, John Stuart Mill (1806-73). Mill and his companion Helen Taylor (1807-58) were close friends of Bessie's parents.

… he broke ranks and described from the inside the process by which boys of his class and culture were conditioned to despise their mothers and sisters as they became men. In **The Subjection of Women** (1869), Mill argued that men and women are fundamentally equal. Only the enormous differences in their upbringing and education accounted for their seemingly different abilities. "What is now called the nature of women is an entirely artificial thing," he wrote. He supported women's equal rights in work, education, property and suffrage, to be won by a mass movement.

The Second Generation: Social Purity Feminism

In the 1870s and 80s, another sort of feminism began to focus on the gaping division between the wife of pure lady-like virtue and the socially outcast prostitute. Only a strong-minded woman of great courage would dare suggest that no difference really existed between them, except for an economic one that made wives and prostitutes sexually available to men on an apparently "different" basis.

IT'S ONLY NATURAL FOR MEN TO SEEK SEXUAL GRATIFICATION. BUT A PROSTITUTE COMMITS AN OFFENCE MOTIVATED BY GAIN!

That's the magistrate who sent me to prison Ma'am - the same who just two days ago gave me money to do his pleasure. It's hard to understand.

Josephine Butler (1828-1906) was a brave pioneer feminist who publicly challenged a male-dominated Victorian society. She took feminism into the streets, workhouses and prisons, and there she gained her insight into the sexual economics of women's subordination.

NOT IN THE LEAST HARD TO

Josephine Butler campaigned vigorously - and often at personal risk - against the British government's Contagious Diseases Act of the 1860s. According to this any working-class woman identified as a prostitute in the areas of barracks and naval ports could be forced into a medical examination by army and navy surgeons.

Josephine was an early member of Langham Place and in touch with American feminists. Women's rights could be won on the political, legal, employment and educational fronts, but for Josephine the question was - would such reforms change the **sexual economics** of women's oppression? Her insistence on the link between economics and sexuality was not welcomed by other emancipationists.

Josephine was entirely modern in denying women's enforced **reproductive** destiny as wives and mothers. She advocated sexual equality that must allow women to operate freely in society without domestic ties. She believed women had a distinctive culture of their own, morally superior to men's.

Social Purity and Temperance - the US Example

The 1870s and 80s also saw the rise of "social purity" feminism, based on Evangelical principles which identified alcohol, violence and sexual excess as the masculine evils threatening women inside the family. Women were believed **different** - morally superior, purer, with little or no need of sex - unlike men who were ruled by animal passions.

WE CLAIM VIRTUE AS OUR OWN, AGAINST MEN WHO ONLY USE THIS WORD HYPOCRITICALLY TO DOMINATE US.

Lucy Stone began to take this conservative view, writing in favour of censorship and expurgated classics in her Boston suffrage paper, **The Women's Journal**, and attacked the actress Sarah Bernhardt as an unmarried mother.

Elizabeth Cady Stanton and Susan Anthony joined the Temperance campaigners. But Elizabeth Cady Stanton disagreed with the "social purity" feminists about women's sexuality. "A healthy woman has as much passion as a man," she declared.

ARMED WITH THE BALLOT, THE MOTHERS OF AMERICA WILL LEGISLATE MORALITY!

Frances Willard (1839-98), leader of the US Women's Christian Temperance Union, campaigned for women's suffrage in order to vote through a prohibition of alcohol.

Some campaigners took to direct action. *Carrie Nation* (1846-1911) left her husband at the age of 21 because of his drinking and brutality. She travelled through Kansas, Illinois, Ohio and New York with a cartload of bricks and axes for smashing up bars. She was a formidable figure, nearly 6 foot tall and weighing over 76 kilos. Carrie produced a broadsheet, **The Smasher's Mail**, and sold souvenir cardboard hatchets.

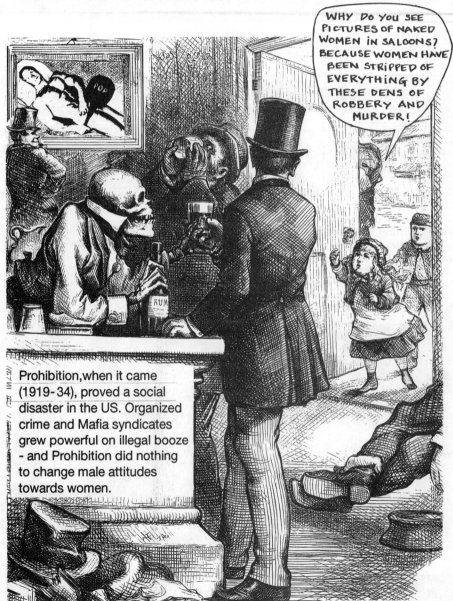

WHY DO YOU SEE PICTURES OF NAKED WOMEN IN SALOONS? BECAUSE WOMEN HAVE BEEN STRIPPED OF EVERYTHING BY THESE DENS OF ROBBERY AND MURDER!

Prohibition, when it came (1919-34), proved a social disaster in the US. Organized crime and Mafia syndicates grew powerful on illegal booze - and Prohibition did nothing to change male attitudes towards women.

The next step was to win the vote. But how? Among the millions who fought for women's suffrage, one family stands out: the Pankhursts - Emmeline and her daughters Christabel and Sylvia. *Emmeline Pankhurst* (1858-1928) grew up in Manchester, then the economic and political heart of Britain, a stronghold of dissent, free trade and radicalism.

FATHER WAS A SELF-MADE MAN, A RADICAL AND SUPPORTER OF PRESIDENT LINCOLN. WHEN I WAS YOUR AGE, I READ THE MORNING PAPER TO HIM AT BREAKFAST... AND WENT COLLECTING MONEY FOR THE FREED BLACK AMERICANS.

Sylvia

Christabel

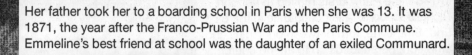

Her father took her to a boarding school in Paris when she was 13. It was 1871, the year after the Franco-Prussian War and the Paris Commune. Emmeline's best friend at school was the daughter of an exiled Communard.

I GREW TO LOVE EVERYTHING FRENCH AND HATE EVERYTHING PRUSSIAN!

Emmeline returned to Manchester in 1878, during the campaign against the government's imperialist policy in the Middle East. The leader of the anti-imperialists was a 39-year-old lawyer, Richard Pankhurst, a reformer who championed trade unionism, an atheist free-thinker, republican and supporter of women's suffrage.

I WAS DETERMINED TO MARRY HIM!

AND IN 1880, I WAS BORN, MY MOTHER'S FAVOURITE... THE ONLY ONE OF 5 CHILDREN THAT SHE EVER NURSED HERSELF.

Christabel

67

In 1883, the Pankhursts moved to London. Richard stood as a left candidate in the East End. Emmeline, torn between principles and ambition, persuaded him to attend church during the campaign. But he lost anyway. Energetic and determined to earn her own money, Emmeline opened a household furnishing shop in 'up and coming' Hampstead Road.

SELLING PASTEL-PAINTED MILK MAID'S STOOLS, ORIENTAL GOODS AND WHITE ENAMELLED WROUGHT-IRON FURNITURE.

The Pankhursts' house in Russell Square was a centre for anarchists, suffragists and women's rights campaigners.

PEOPLE LIKE WILLIAM MORRIS, TOM MANN AND ANNIE BESANT...

AND LOUISE MICHEL, THE FAMOUS PETROLEUSE OF THE PARIS COMMUNE, LIKE A FAIRY-TALE CHARACTER.

Women's suffrage was often discussed. Richard asked:

WHY ARE WOMEN SO PATIENT? WHY DON'T YOU SCRATCH OUR EYES OUT AND FORCE US TO GIVE YOU THE VOTE?

Sylvia felt picked upon.

Christabel was always confident and being worshipped. She dominated even Emmeline who felt afraid of her. When the girls joined the Clarion cycling club, Emmeline made sure Christabel got the best bike in the catalogue, a magnificent machine costing £30.

In 1894, the Pankhursts moved back to Manchester. They had money troubles and Richard's health was suffering, though he kept it secret. He and Emmeline, now convinced socialists, joined the far-left Independent Labour Party with Keir Hardie. Of all the left groups, the ILP was the most sympathetic to feminism; many of its best speakers were women.

I SAW MY FATHER CAMPAIGNING HIMSELF TO DEATH.

Richard died suddenly in 1897 of an ulcerated stomach.

DAMNED IF I'LL DEPEND ON CHARITY! I'LL OPEN ANOTHER SHOP.

I WON A SCHOLARSHIP TO ART SCHOOL AND LATER ONE TO VENICE, DESPITE MY POOR HEALTH AND WEAK EYES.

AND I'M STUDYING TO BE A LAWYER.

Emmeline

Christabel

Sylvia

Christabel joined with other young socialist feminists in Manchester. In 1901 she met *Eva Gore Booth*, younger sister of *Constance Markievicz*, a leader in the Irish uprising of 1916, the first woman elected to Parliament (although as a Sinn Fein supporter she didn't take her seat).

EVA IS A TRADE UNION ACTIVIST AND GIVES EVENING CLASSES ON SHAKESPEARE TO WOMEN TEXTILE WORKERS.

JOIN US IN THE MANCHESTER WOMEN'S TRADE COUNCILS AND FIGHT FOR WOMEN'S SUFFRAGE.

The unions were beginning to run their own Parliamentary candidates - and this was the forerunner of the Labour Party. Women made up the majority of the textile unions, but because they had no votes were held of no account.

By 1902, 3,000 women textile workers in Yorkshire alone had signed petitions for the vote!

Annie Kenney (1879-1953) worked in the mills from the age of 10 and had one of her fingers torn off by the machinery. She became Christabel's loyal lieutenant, encouraging her to speak on soap-boxes at village fairs. Christabel soon learned to answer hecklers and developed a powerful style.

1903: the WSPU

Emmeline was elected ILP candidate to the Manchester School Board in 1901, but grew impatient with the ILP's dithering on women's suffrage. She set up the rival Women's Social and Political Union in 1903 in her Nelson Street parlour.

FOR 20 YEARS, SINCE J.S. MILL FIRST PRESENTED THE LANGHAM PLACE PETITION TO PARLIAMENT, BILLS FOR WOMEN'S SUFFRAGE HAVE BEEN VOTED DOWN. THERE HAS TO BE A CHANGE OF TACTICS!

These were turbulent times. Germany and the USA were competing against British goods in foreign markets. The long decline of British industry was beginning as British capital was invested more profitably overseas. A new trade unionism was spreading among the mass of unskilled workers, amid growing industrial unrest.

AND WOMEN PLAYED A VITAL PART IN AGITATION.

THE BRITISH SUFFRAGE MOVEMENT WAS A WORKING WOMEN'S MOVEMENT AS NEVER BEFORE!

WOMEN'S SOCIAL AND POLITICAL

72

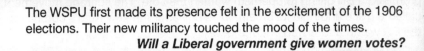

The WSPU first made its presence felt in the excitement of the 1906 elections. Their new militancy touched the mood of the times.
Will a Liberal government give women votes?

But in 1907, Christabel and Emmeline broke with the ILP and the Labour parliamentary campaign.

The WSPU grew massively. 3,000 branches sprang up in 1907, drawing in teachers, shopgirls, clerks, dressmakers and textile workers. Their newspaper, **Votes for Women,** sold 40,000 copies a week. Women's suffrage meetings filled the Albert Hall. 250,000 attended a demonstration in Hyde Park.

In 1911, victory seemed within grasp. Prime Minister Asquith had virtually promised a Bill giving (propertied) women the vote. The suffrage movement called a truce and held its breath. In 1912 - after the new King's coronation - the Bill was manoeuvred out of the way.

ASQUITH WANTED TO MAKE SURE THAT NO DEMONSTRATIONS WOULD DISRUPT THE CORONATION...

HE HAD NO INTENTION OF GIVING US THE VOTE!

Our opponents care more for their property than for women? Very well - let's attack their property, not people.

Crash! went the windows of the Home Office, War Office, Foreign Office, the Board of Trade, the Treasury and the National Liberal Club. Shop windows were smashed all over the West End.

Arrests, Hunger Strikes and Force-Feeding

Hundreds of suffragettes were arrested. When they protested with hunger strikes, the oral rape of force-feeding was inflicted on them.
When the public outcry against this torture grew too embarrassing, the Liberal Government introduced the "Cat and Mouse Act". Women on hunger strike would be released when their health deteriorated, only to be re-arrested when they recovered sufficiently.

Emmeline, now 55, was dragged off to Holloway gaol a dozen times. Small, frail but fearless, she conducted her own defence.

WHAT DO YOU SAY M'LORD, ABOUT THE EMINENT JUDGE OF ASSIZES FOUND DEAD THIS MORNING IN A BROTHEL?

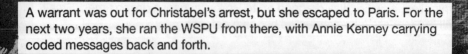

A warrant was out for Christabel's arrest, but she escaped to Paris. For the next two years, she ran the WSPU from there, with Annie Kenney carrying coded messages back and forth.

A WOMEN'S MOVEMENT IN THE EAST END'S GREAT ABYSS OF POVERTY IS A MODEL FOR THE ENTIRE COUNTRY.

Each time the state stepped up its violence against the suffragettes, Christabel decreed an increase of theirs. Soon there were arson attacks as well as window smashings. Many WSPU members were unhappy with a tactic that alienated supporters and played into the government's hands. Sylvia preferred to carry on with the old methods of mass protest in East London.

Labour militancy was at its height. In 1911, the dockers and transport workers' strike brought the country to a standstill. In Bermondsey, just south of the Thames, striking women workers from a food factory were joined by 15,000 others from local factories and workshops at a meeting in Southwark Park. They wanted better wages - and the **vote** too!

Early in 1914, Sylvia was summoned to a meeting with Emmeline and Christabel in Paris. Her health was poor - she too had had her share of prison and hunger strikes. Only Christabel looked <u>rosy</u> and strong as ever. And she demanded that the East London Federation withdraw from the WSPU.

WHY?

Because working women are the weakest of our sex, their lives too hard, their education too meagre to equip them for this contest. We want only the very best pick, able to march in step like an army.

SHE CARES MORE FOR THAT LAP-DOG THAN ME.

Emmeline tried to intervene.

Sylvia was forced to accept.

PERHAPS WE CAN COMPROMISE ON SYLVIA'S EAST END WOMEN...

NO! IT MUST BE A CLEAN CUT!

I'm too ill and tired to fight and I need money.

As Sylvia got up to leave, Christabel softened a little.

PERHAPS WE CAN MEET SOMETIMES AS SISTERS AND NOT AS SUFFRAGETTES.

MEANINGLESS WORDS - WE HAVE NO LIFE OUTSIDE OF THE MOVEMENT.

Six months later World War One began - and Sylvia was glad of the "clean cut". Emmeline and Christabel were suddenly transformed into patriots - the WSPU's paper was renamed **Britannia** and its motto was now "King, Country, Freedom".

Sylvia was totally opposed to the war. In 1915, she attended the anti-war International Women's Congress for peace, called by *Aletta Jacobs* (1854-1929), a Dutch socialist feminist and her country's first woman doctor. Sylvia joined the anti-war Women's International League and went on helping East End women, now drafted into "men's jobs" in engineering and armaments factories, to get the same pay as men.

The British government, weakened by the War, broke down before the onslaught of the women. In 1918 women over 30 won the right to vote.

It had taken four generations of hard struggle for women to battle their way into the political arena. Now, at last, we had got there!

SO LOOK OUT, BOYS, WE'RE COMING!

Worldwide 19th Century Women's Movements

Women were winning the vote - not just in Britain but in many other countries worldwide. In Canada, the USA, Germany, Sweden - and in Norway where Henrik Ibsen's plays (**A Doll's House** 1879, **The Wild Duck** 1884, **Hedda Gabler** 1890) had protested against women's subjection.

In **India,** women's rights campaigners were fighting for girls' right to education, for Home Rule and the vote. In 1918, they won the support of the Indian National Congress. The Women's Indian Association lobbied the Viceroy and sent a delegation to Britain to press their claim. *Pandita Ramabai* (1858-1922), one of the foremost Sanskrit scholars of her generation, wrote a feminist study of Hinduism, **Women's Religious Law.** Widowed at the age of 24 and with a daughter to care for, she travelled the country founding a series of women's organizations, *Mahila Samaj*, and was one of an influential group of feminists inside the Indian National Congress.

In **Indonesia,** *Raden Ajen Kartini* (1879-1904), daughter of a high official, spoke out against polygyny, forced marriage and colonial oppression, and argued for women's right to education. She started a girls' school of 120 students - but died tragically in childbirth at the age of 25.

In **Japan,** pioneering feminist *Kishida Toshiko* (1863-1901) led 19th century campaigns for women's rights and suffrage. The feminist "bluestocking" group **Seitoscha** published a magazine, **Seito** (1911-16), with articles on contemporary culture, marriage, women's rights and suffrage. The first women's suffrage campaign was set up in 1917.

In **China,** *Tan Junying* founded the Chinese Suffragette Society in Beijing in 1911 and led women's demonstrations to picket national Assembly meetings.

Australian women won the vote as early as 1909 (although aboriginal Australian women did not get it until 1967). The Australian Women's Political Association was founded in 1909, campaigning for equal pay and equal rights. The **Brazilian** Federation for the Advancement of Women, founded by Bertha Lutz in 1922, won women's suffrage in 1932. The first International Feminist Congress was held in **Argentina** in 1910. In 1918, a national Feminist Party was set up there, and from 1919 the 11,000-strong Women's Rights Organization campaigned for the right to vote.

SOCIALIST FEMINISM

But could the situation of women ever be improved unless the poverty and exploitation that most women suffered were done away with? Growing numbers of women were joining the huge new socialist movements. An early socialist feminist was *Flora Tristan* (1803-44), the illegitimate daughter of a Spanish Peruvian father and French mother. Flora grew up penniless and worked as an engraver's colourist. In Paris, she discovered the ancient craft unions, the **compagnonnages,** which inspired her most influential work, **The Workers' Union** (1843).

I HAVE NEARLY THE WHOLE WORLD AGAINST ME. MEN BECAUSE I DEMAND THE EMANCIPATION OF WOMEN; THE OWNERS BECAUSE I DEMAND THE EMANCIPATION OF WAGE-EARNERS!

Flora based her programme for a workers' union on two plans. (1) Workers in every country would contribute to a fund for the self-emancipation of labour. (2) The fund would establish communal "workers' palaces" combining the self-governing functions of hospital, home for the aged, schools and centres of advanced studies. Women would gain their emancipation in these communities of "Human Unity".

Flora's scheme is called **Utopian Socialist** because of its links with the ideas of workers' model communities envisaged by such pioneer socialists as Robert Owen (1771-1858) and François-Marie-Charles Fourier (1772-1837).

Flora's ideas were taken up by a group of socialist feminists in Paris during the 1848 revolution.

Paul Gauguin

HISTORICAL MATERIALISM &

Since Wollstonecraft's time, feminists had believed that the subordinate position of women was neither "natural" nor inevitable, but socially created. But they had no evidence to argue against the dominant religious view that God had created women as "secondary and inferior" creatures out of Adam's rib.

By the 1880s, Darwin's theory of biological evolution and the discoveries made by the new science of anthropology could be combined for the first time to explain **how** women became subordinate to men.

Friedrich Engels (1820-95), revolutionary socialist, writer and activist, was a staunch supporter of women's rights and suffrage.

THE WOMEN'S CAUSE

Engels' book, **The Origins of the Family, Private Property and the State** (1884) used ethnographic and historical evidence to show that women's social position had not always been inferior.

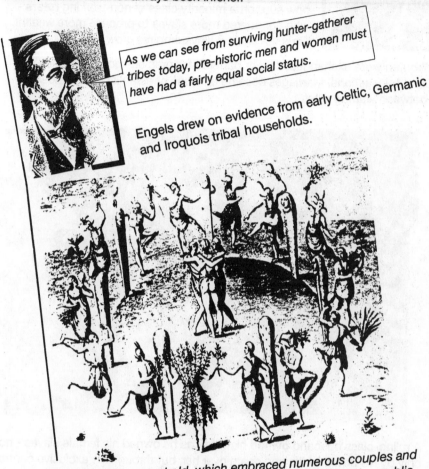

As we can see from surviving hunter-gatherer tribes today, pre-historic men and women must have had a fairly equal social status.

Engels drew on evidence from early Celtic, Germanic and Iroquois tribal households.

*"In the old, communistic household, which embraced numerous couples and their children, the administration of the household was just as much a public, socially necessary industry as the procurement of food. With the development of the modern individual family, the administration of the household lost its public character. It became a **private** service and the wife became the first **domestic** servant, pushed out of participation in social production."*

Engels traced the enforced subordination of women back to the origins of private property in ancient times.

From about 5000 B.C., civilizations based on agriculture developed in the fertile areas of the Tigris and Euphrates, the Nile, Indus and Mekong rivers. Humankind began to produce significantly more than was needed for the tribe to stay alive and reproduce itself. A **surplus** of food could now support a minority class of non-working **rulers** - who conquered more slaves to produce more wealth! Thus the ancient slave empires grew.

Women were exchanged, sold or bartered for precious goods, treaties and land transactions. Marriages became a means of establishing alliances between warring elites.

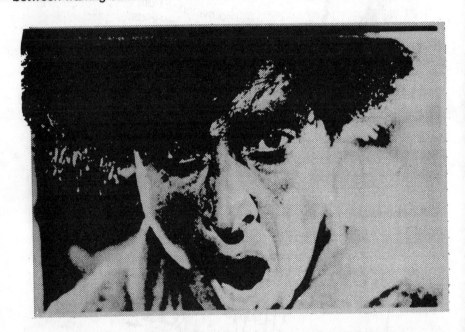

A ruling-class husband **owned** his wife - as he owned his female slaves - not only by his power of life and death over her, but through his exclusive control over her **fertility**. The veiling and seclusion of women, the cult of virginity and the death penalty for women's adultery (never for men) are all evidence of men's total control over women's life, freedom of movement, sexuality and death.

Some of the anthropological data Engels used has been disproved now - but his insights into the links between the economic structure of a society and the family forms it adopts are still fascinating!

I saw that modern industry gave women the opportunity to participate in social production again.

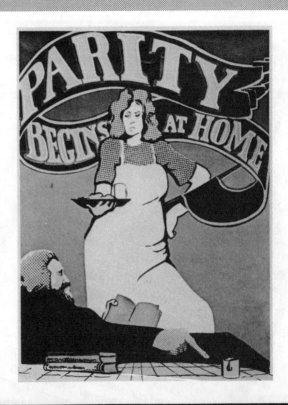

"But only in such a way that, if she fulfils her duties in the private service of her family, she is excluded from production and cannot earn anything; and if she wishes to take part in public industry and earn her living independently, she is not in a position to fulfil her family duties. What applies to the woman in the factory applies to her in all branches of business, right up to medicine and law. The modern domestic family is based on the overt and covert domestic slavery of women."

FEMINISM AND GERMAN

Engels' ideas were immediately adopted by the German Social Democratic Party, an influential socialist party that arose in late 19th century Germany.

In 1883, SDP leader Auguste Bebel published **Woman under Socialism,** a world best-seller that popularized and extended the work of Engels.

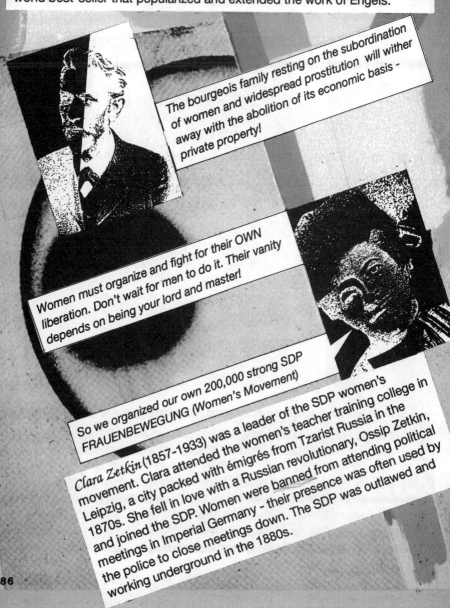

The bourgeois family resting on the subordination of women and widespread prostitution will wither away with the abolition of its economic basis - private property!

Women must organize and fight for their OWN liberation. Don't wait for men to do it. Their vanity depends on being your lord and master!

So we organized our own 200,000 strong SDP FRAUENBEWEGUNG (Women's Movement)

Clara Zetkin (1857-1933) was a leader of the SDP women's movement. Clara attended the women's teacher training college in Leipzig, a city packed with émigrés from Tzarist Russia in the 1870s. She fell in love with a Russian revolutionary, Ossip Zetkin, and joined the SDP. Women were banned from attending political meetings in Imperial Germany - their presence was often used by the police to close meetings down. The SDP was outlawed and working underground in the 1880s.

Ossip was deported from Germany with the clampdown of the 1880s. The couple lived in Paris till Ossip's death in 1889. Widowed at 32, with two young sons to support, Clara became one of the chief organizers of the SDP's women's movement on her return to Germany after the anti-socialist laws were lifted in 1890.

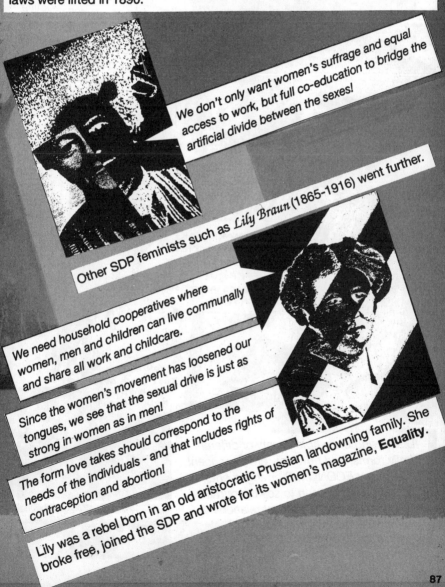

We don't only want women's suffrage and equal access to work, but full co-education to bridge the artificial divide between the sexes!

Other SDP feminists such as *Lily Braun* (1865-1916) went further.

We need household cooperatives where women, men and children can live communally and share all work and childcare.

Since the women's movement has loosened our tongues, we see that the sexual drive is just as strong in women as in men!

The form love takes should correspond to the needs of the individuals - and that includes rights of contraception and abortion!

Lily was a rebel born in an old aristocratic Prussian landowning family. She broke free, joined the SDP and wrote for its women's magazine, **Equality**.

 # AND IN RUSSIA...

Meanwhile, the Russian revolution had occurred and a workers' state had been created for the first time - but in the worst possible conditions, at the end of World War One, in a devastated and backward country threatened by famine and civil war. At a time like this, Lenin asked Clara Zetkin in 1920...

Why are SDP women devoting so much time to discussions about sex? Surely there are more important questions for socialist women to discuss than the marriage forms of the Maori or the theories of Sigmund Freud?

SEX AND MARRIAGE IN THIS ROTTEN SOCIETY INVOLVE REAL CONFLICT, REAL SUFFERING FOR WOMEN OF ALL RANKS AND SOCIAL CLASSES.

YOU SOUND JUST LIKE OUR COMRADE KOLLONTAI!

Discussing the whole history of different family forms, and how they are dependent on different ECONOMIC arrangements, helps working women to see beyond the superstition that the present relations of capitalist society are eternal.

COMRADE KOLLONTAI AND THE HOPES OF SOVIET RUSSIA

Alexandra Kollontai was born into a landowning Finno-Russian family. Beautiful, fiery and independent, she married young - against her family's wishes - to a cousin, Vladimir Kollontai. The turning point in Alexandra's life came in 1896, when she accompanied Vladimir, a factory inspector, on one of his visits.

Vladimir was complacent but Alexandra was outraged and soon joined a Marxist group in support of the 1896 St. Petersburg textile workers' strike. Vladimir tried to prevent her. Alexandra was bitterly torn, but in the end decided to leave him, and temporarily her son.

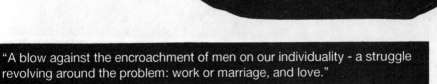

"A blow against the encroachment of men on our individuality - a struggle revolving around the problem: work or marriage, and love."

Alexandra's activities in a socialist women's group drew the attention of the Tzarist police and she had to flee Russia. Exiled in Europe and the USA, she fought passionately against the advent of the First World War. In 1914 she joined Lenin's Bolshevik Party, the War's strongest opponents. With the February Revolution of 1917, she returned to Russia. Seven months later, after the victory of the Bolshevik's October Revolution, Lenin brought her into his government as Commissar for Social Welfare.

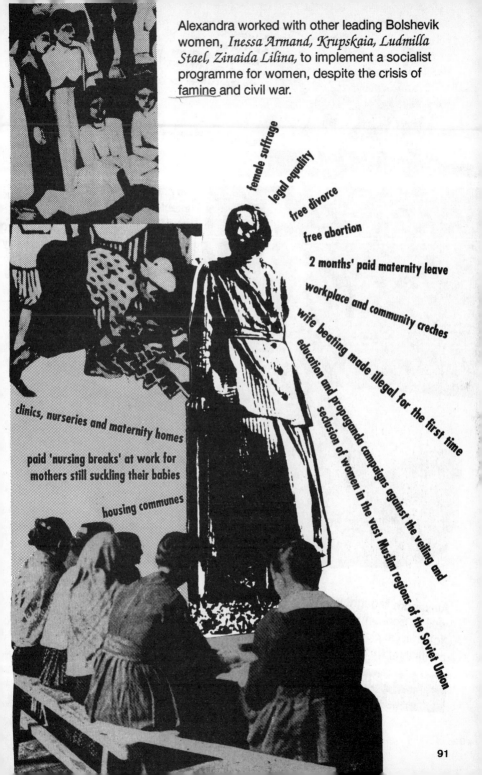

Alexandra worked with other leading Bolshevik women, *Inessa Armand, Krupskaia, Ludmilla Stael, Zinaida Lilina,* to implement a socialist programme for women, despite the crisis of famine and civil war.

female suffrage

legal equality

free divorce

free abortion

2 months' paid maternity leave

workplace and community creches

wife beating made illegal for the first time

education and propaganda campaigns against the veiling and seclusion of women in the vast Muslim regions of the Soviet Union

clinics, nurseries and maternity homes

paid 'nursing breaks' at work for mothers still suckling their babies

housing communes

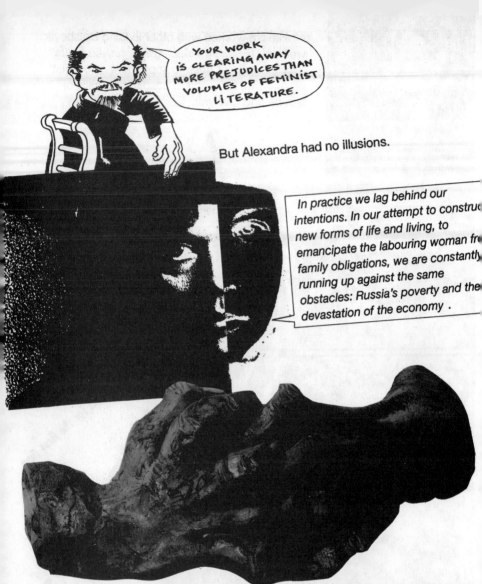

YOUR WORK IS CLEARING AWAY MORE PREJUDICES THAN VOLUMES OF FEMINIST LITERATURE.

But Alexandra had no illusions.

In practice we lag behind our intentions. In our attempt to construct new forms of life and living, to emancipate the labouring woman from family obligations, we are constantly running up against the same obstacles: Russia's poverty and the devastation of the economy .

Alexandra brought women's struggles for freedom - sexual and emotional as well as economic - to the very heart of the socialist revolution. She turned to fiction to explore the experiences of the "new woman" grappling with the conflicting demands of work and love, suffering passion and independence.

No wonder that for socialist feminists of the 1960s and 70s, Alexandra was no distant historical figure but a true friend and sister-in-arms!

THE 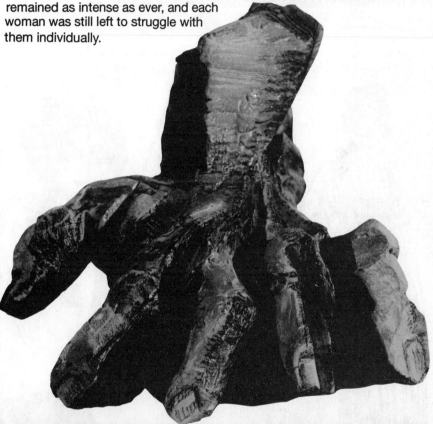 BACKLASH

Very few of the extraordinary reforms achieved by communist feminists survived the Stalinist backlash of the 1930s, although the verbal commitment to women's suffrage remained. Millions of women were brought into the labour force, but the problems of combining work with having children remained as intense as ever, and each woman was still left to struggle with them individually.

Under **Stalin**, the early great hopes for new ways of living and loving were brought to an end. "Strengthening the family" was made an official task, "free love" was denounced as a bourgeois invention. In an effort to solve the short-fall of the labour force at women's expense, the "Order of Maternal Glory" was introduced as a reward for mothers of seven children or more. Anti-abortion and anti-divorce laws were passed in 1936, and homosexuality was outlawed.

The Roaring 20s...

Most girls in Europe and North America now received primary school education. Upper middle-class ones were forcing their way into the universities and professions. Women played a big role in the Harlem "renaissance" and the cultural avant garde of the 20s. Job opportunities provided millions of young women with a new independent way of life. Feminism began to seem old-fashioned, a relic of past struggles.

...and the Hungry 30s

The 20s ended with a worldwide economic Crash. Rulers in Europe and Japan turned to the fascist parties to restore "order" amid the growing unrest. As the Great Depression of the 30s deepened, jobs grew fewer and were bitterly contested. Women were resented for "stealing" men's work.

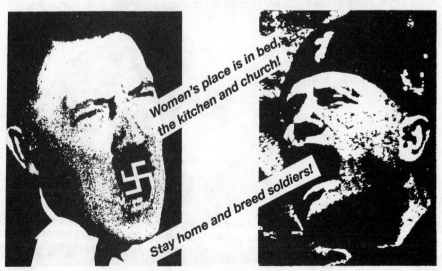

Then came World War II (1939-45)...

Suddenly, the rules changed. In the US, 7 million women went to work for the first time, as men marched off to fight. Women took up jobs they "couldn't do"...

Overnight, governments found money for day-care centres and nurseries.

The Tranquillizer 50s

At the end of the war, 4 out of 5 women in the US wanted to keep their jobs in peacetime. Men thought different. Job segregation returned with a vengeance. In the 50s women were constantly brainwashed by ads, movies and vulgarized psychoanalysis to stay home and be happy housewives.

Your pay isn't important.

Work doesn't matter to you.

Well-adjusted women care only about their husbands and children – not themselves.

Bad mothers are to blame for crime, delinquency, alcoholism - and for men's sexual worries, inadequacies and homosexuality!

Howling in the Wilderness

Simone de Beauvoir (1908-86) was a lone feminist voice in the 50s. She broke with her Catholic upper-middle-class background in the 30s to become a radical intellectual and novelist - and to live an independent life in Paris.

Simone's book **The Second Sex** (1949) was an encyclopaedic work, drawing on history, biology, psychoanalysis, Marxism and literature. Ironic, intelligent, full of humour and good sense, it lay ticking like a time-bomb, waiting for a new generation of rebellious women to discover when they burst upon the scene.

The New Left Women

Increasing numbers of college-educated women in the US and Europe now had raised expectations. They **felt** equal - but in practice still found themselves trapped in the traditional secondary role of looking after men and striving for their attention and approval.

It's one thing being screwed over by capitalist pigs - but it's something else to be screwed over by the "liberators of the human race"!

"Cool down, little girl"

The last straw came in the summer of 1967 when a conference on New Politics in Chicago dropped the feminists' resolution from their agenda.

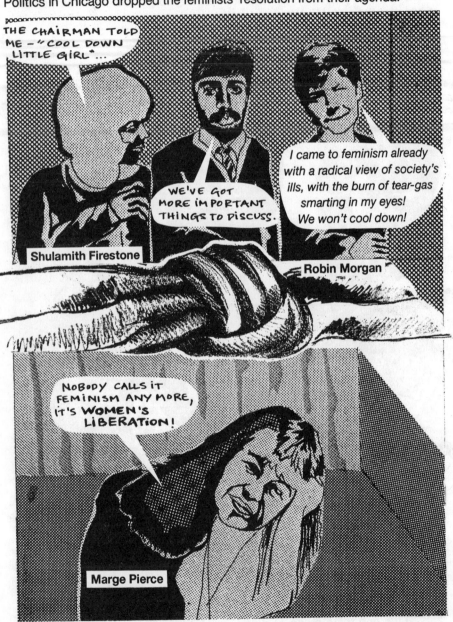

THE CHAIRMAN TOLD ME — "COOL DOWN LITTLE GIRL"...

WE'VE GOT MORE IMPORTANT THINGS TO DISCUSS.

I came to feminism already with a radical view of society's ills, with the burn of tear-gas smarting in my eyes! We won't cool down!

Shulamith Firestone

Robin Morgan

NOBODY CALLS IT FEMINISM ANY MORE, IT'S WOMEN'S LIBERATION!

Marge Pierce

Zapping Miss America, 1968

One of the first actions of the women's liberation groups was to protest at the annual "Miss America" Beauty Contest. The idea grew out of a "rap group" in New York. Women came from Canada, Florida and all over the East Coast to perform non-stop guerrilla theatre in the street outside the contest hall.

They crowned a sheep "Miss America" (with lots of baa-ing) and set up a Freedom Trash Can for a whole load of objects symbolic of women's oppression.

"Bra-burning women's libbers!" screamed the press the next day. A new myth was born - although nothing in the Freedom Trash Can had actually gone up in smoke!

Consciousness Raising

Women began meeting by themselves in "consciousness raising" groups. Radical husbands and male comrades reacted angrily at first to these new women-only meetings.

WHY SHOULD MEN BE EXCLUDED?

IT'S A BOURGEOIS, SELF-INDULGENT DIVERSION!

WHAT DO YOU DO THERE?

Just a simple fact - the atmosphere was **different** in women-only meetings. It was lighter somehow. Women talked more freely and made more discoveries about themselves when men weren't around. Things they'd never realized or said aloud before were facets of a common experience.

OUR EXPERIENCE WAS NOT ON ANYBODY'S AGENDA.

WE WERE STILL WORKING IT OUT FOR OURSELVES.

These rap groups of the 60s' counter-culture had many models - Cuban women's committees, the "Speaking Bitterness" meetings of peasants in the Chinese revolution, and the age-old habit of women talking around the kitchen table.

Betty Friedan, resigning from the presidency of NOW in 1970, called for a Women's Strike to mark the 50th anniversary of the 19th Amendment that gave women the right to vote. The amount of support the Women's Strike attracted took everyone by surprise, not least its organizers. The idea had wide press coverage, but that alone could not account for the thousands of women all across the US coming together on the campuses, in school groups and in neighbourhood groups.

1970 was the year the US women's liberation movement really took off. Ahead lay years of struggle, songs and arguments, victories and defeats. The Equal Rights Amendment to the US Constitution, outlawing sex discrimination, was passed by the Senate in 1972 (it failed to win ratification by a majority of State legislatures, however, and fell in 1982). In 1973, the historic **Roe vs. Wade** Supreme Court decision gave women the right to choose on abortion.

By 1973, a women's liberation directory listed over 2,000 groups in the USA, from consciousness-raising groups to women's karate classes, from self-help health groups and campaigns for free abortion and contraception to women's history studies, from Congressional lobbyists to street theatre groups, from legal advice centres to followers of the Goddess, and a whole new lesbian movement. There were women's caucuses in the trade unions, a National Organization of Black Feminists, Chicana groups, Native American women's groups and even a group of feminist nuns doing abortion referral work.

Sisterhood and Difference

The sudden explosion of a new mass movement brought a number of different experiences into conflict, clashes were inevitable - and often painful. This was due in part to the youth of the movement, an over-zealous attention to what was "correct" and a lack of experience in allowing different viewpoints to co-exist. Valuable new ideas turned dogmatic and exclusive when pushed to their logical extremes - or beyond.

But the differences reflected the real, social divisions that existed between women in a society bitterly riven by class and race as well as sex.

Black Women's Liberation

For many women in the black liberation movement, the rediscovery of their African heritage was strengthening and invigorating - but also brought problems of difference to the surface.

These early years of the women's movement were also a time when the US government resorted to physical extermination of the Black Power movement. Police attacked their offices with automatic weapons. Leading Black Panthers were gunned down in their beds. Black Panther women in prison were giving birth under armed guard, their babies immediately snatched from them.

WE WERE CONSTANTLY DODGING BULLETS AND WONDERING WHOSE FUNERAL WE'D BE ATTENDING NEXT!

In prison, Angela Davis began researching the hidden history of black women and their role during slavery. She raised questions about the position of women in the movement and about the stereotypes of black women as all-powerful, all-providing mother and as domineering, castrating matriarch.

FEMINISM IS DIVIDING OUR MOVEMENT AND DOING THE WHITE MAN'S JOB FOR HIM.

RACISM HAS EMASCULATED AFRO-AMERICAN MEN LONG ENOUGH!

NOW THAT WE ARE FINDING OUR PRIDE AGAIN IT'S YOUR JOB TO STAND BY US.

Lesbian Liberation

Lesbian feminists added the challenge of another sort of difference. Women living and loving independently from men raised the immediate question of women's relationship to the heterosexual male-dominated nuclear family.

Psychiatry in the 1900s tried to categorize lesbians as unfortunate "inverts".

The Well of Loneliness (1928) by the lesbian novelist, Radclyffe Hall, did most to popularize this view of creatures "born into the wrong bodies", doomed to a life of torment and morbidity.

I MEANT IT AS A PLEA TO LEAVE US IN PEACE, RATHER THAN BE FORCIBLY "CURED".

Ironically, Radclyffe Hall was part of a flourishing lesbian culture in the 20s Bohemia.

We were a privileged minority

Lesbians in the early 60s had to disguise **their** feelings or be penalized for them.

The infant women's movement of the 60s mostly focussed on heterosexuality, often militantly so.

NOW will lose all public support if it's seen to be tainted by the "lavender menace" of lesbianism.

What! ? We're the most conscious "woman-centred" women in the movement, and you ignore or deny our experience?

Some feminists considered their lesbianism was more than a sexual preference. It was a social and political choice to turn one's life, love and energy towards women, rather than waste all that on a relationship with a man. "Political lesbians" asked a pertinent and embarrassing question.

Are heterosexual women sleeping in the enemy camp?

Lesbian Mothers

The movement did help many women to "come out" and refocus their lives. But some new "out" lesbians were shocked to find their fellow-feminists unwilling even to talk about the problems they faced.

Lesbian mothers faced homophobic prejudice and hostility which affected them in housing, childcare and jobs.

A British Model of Women's Liberation

Spring 1968 - a time of protest and hope around the world.

At the Ford Motor Company's plant in Dagenham, east London, the women sewing-machinists were talking about a strike.

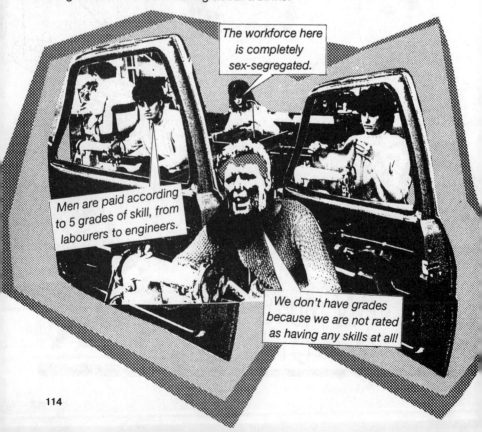

The sewing-machinists were upholsterers who made the cars' seats. It was detailed work that took concentration and a lot of manual dexterity and it strained the back and eyes.

The strike brought the whole factory to a standstill. "The rate for the job" was a fundamental principle of the British workers' movement. The Ford women, militant, articulate and brave, went on TV to argue their case, against more hostility than support from sulky, laid-off male Ford workers. Other women took courage from their stand and there was a rash of "equal pay" strikes across the country.

Audrey Wise was a typist working for a mail-order company. She had a baby and a husband dismissed from his factory for trade union organizing. Audrey was an instinctive, independent-minded feminist who came from generations of socialist trade unionists in Newcastle upon Tyne.

We embarked on something bigger than our union and our own factory.

Our strike touched the condition of all working women and sparked off a national upheaval.

So we decided to set up NJACCWER - the National Joint Action Campaign Committee for Women's Equal Rights.

Audrey was one of the speakers at the big Equal Pay rally that NJACCWER organized in 1969 in Trafalgar Square. It was Sunday and pouring with rain.

"Of course the discussion centred on equal pay. But as with everything to do with women, it can never stay on wages. There's no boundaries, ever. I could imagine the conversations going on in people's houses - 'I'm going to London. How can we afford it? What about the dinner? Who will look after the children?' Whereas a man would simply say, 'I'm going on a demonstration.' I looked out from the platform to these thousands of women - and I thought of all the Sunday dinners gone uncooked."

From the start, the British women's movement had a stronger working-class and socialist feminist element to it than the US one, although the US movement was better organized, better resourced and - some felt - far more feisty.

From the late 60s and 70s came an impressive upsurge of intellectual and militant activity by a first generation of women liberationists in Britain.

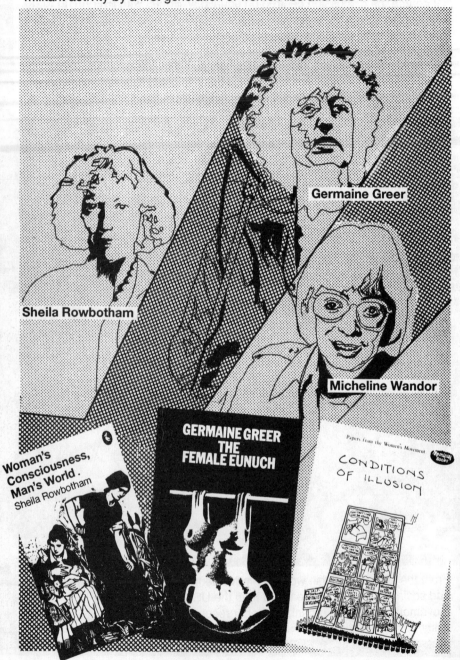

Germaine Greer

Sheila Rowbotham

Micheline Wandor

Woman's Consciousness, Man's World.
Sheila Rowbotham

GERMAINE GREER
THE FEMALE EUNUCH

Papers from the Women's Movement
CONDITIONS OF ILLUSION

A women's group at a History Workshop meeting at Ruskin Trade Union College, Oxford, decided to call the first conference on women's liberation in 1970 - the real beginning of the British women's movement.

NO REVOLUTION WITHOUT WOMEN'S LIBERATION!

600 of us crowded into the Oxford Union building where less than 10 years before we had been forbidden to speak.

There was excitement, revelation and muddle...

And arguments with maoists and Situationists who were spraying the wall!

There was a creche run by men.

Three main tendencies in the

The women's movement swiftly grew into a major political force, spreading across Europe and North America. Different tendencies developed within the movement as it grew - **radical feminists, social feminists and liberal or "equal opportunity" feminists.**

Radical feminists: We radical feminists see the problem as **patriarchy** - a whole system of male power over women. Male rulers, male military, industrial, political and religious establishments, male trade unions and the male-dominated left are all apart of the patriarchy...reinforcing - and reinforced by - the power of individual men over women and children within their families.

Women are one class, men are another!

Socialist feminists: How can you say Mrs. Henry Ford IV is really in the same class as a Guatemalan peasant woman? We socialist feminists see the problem as a combination of male domination *and* class exploitation - our fight is against both! Real liberation is impossible as long as power and wealth in the world is monopolized by a tiny minority, and economic and social life is ruled by their lust for profits.

Liberal feminists: You girls always go too far! The problem is simply one of prejudice - the system needs to be corrected, not overturned. What we need is more equal-rights legislation, more positive role models to give girls confidence.

Each tendency stressed different **strategies** for the fight.

Women's Movement, 1970-79

Radical feminists: Stressed women only campaigns and demonstrations, building a women's space and a women's culture. They concentrated on the sharp end of male/female relations - campaigning especially against men's violence against women, rape and pornography.

Socialist feminists: Put more emphasis on making alliances with other oppressed groups and classes - anti-imperialist movements, workers' organizations, the political parties of the left. They were engaged in a permanent dialogue - sometimes exhausting, sometimes exhilarating - with progressive men in these organizations about the meaning and importance of the feminist struggle, about the way gender oppression is reflected and reinforced within personal and family relationships - and within the very structure of liberation movements and parties.

Liberal feminists: A smaller group - concentrated on lobbying governments for pro-women reforms and trying to influence the decision makers. All too often, however they were fobbed off with declarations and resolutions that meant nothing in practice.

The **socialist feminists** predominated in the women's movement to begin with, as it emerged out of the social protests and anti-Vietnam war movement of the late 1960s. By the end of the 1970s, the **radical feminists** had grown more influential.

In the more conservative 1990s, there has been a growing together of different positions into a synthesis that recognizes some of the strengths and weaknesses in all three tendencies - and sees feminism as an ally of all human rights'movements against militarism, authoritarianism and tyranny.

Black Women Organizing

The late 70s saw a dramatic stepping-up of the British government's harassment of black people. Deportations, airport detentions and the "Sus" laws gave police new powers to "stop and search". There was a general criminalization of people of Afro-Caribbean and Asian descent. This mood encouraged far-right racist attacks.

Black feminists played a vital role in organizing militant self-defence groups the Brixton Black Women's Centre, Southall Black Sisters, Manchester Black Women's Cooperative and other community campaigns. In 1978 these black groups, together with women students from Zimbabwe, Ghana, Ethiopia, Eritrea and other countries, called a national conference in London.They set up a coordinating network, OWWAD, the Organization of Women of Asian and African Descent.

Women against Fundamentalism

Organizing against rape and domestic violence brought these black and Asian women into conflict with the traditional male leaders of their communities - and also with the black and white anti-racists and multiculturalists who had allied themselves to those traditional leaderships. The tension grew in the 80s as the fundamentalist leaderships - all sharing a rigidly patriarchal view of the role of women - tried to assert their authority within the ethnic communities.

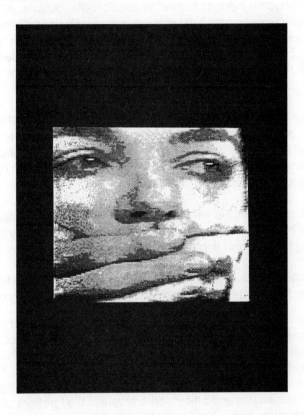

Feminists from widely different backgrounds - Iranian oppositionists, Indian anti-communalists, Israeli anti-Zionists and Irish anti-clerics - organized **Women against Fundamentalism.** On International Women's Day, 1990, WAF organized a meeting on worldwide fundamentalism, with women delegates from Bangladesh, Britain, Iran, Israel, Ghana, the US and USSR

Women around the World

The woman's movement is a global one.

In **Germany** the theoretical influence of the far left and of radical psychoanalytical thinking was very strong in the 60s women's liberation movement. Feminist magazines (**Courage, Emma**) flourished in the 70s. There was a big campaign against the abortion law, **Paragraph 218**, with the slogan, "My womb belongs to me!" Women's cafés, centres, bookshops, lesbian collectives and feminist action groups proliferated. Green politics were a big influence on feminism in the 80s - and feminism on green politics. In the late 80s, a big debate erupted over the **Mothers' Manifesto**, which argued for the superiority of "womanly values" over "masculine" ones in social, political and economic life.

In **Italy**, feminists started a radio station, **Radio Donna**, and **Effe** magazine. In Naples, cashiers in department stores and supermarkets went on a "Smile Strike", refusing to act "pleasing" to the customers until pay and conditions were improved. Massive campaigns for freer divorce, abortion rights and against rape led to important changes in the law.

In **France**, prostitutes led a nationwide campaign of sit-ins in cathedrals and town halls in 1976, protesting against the male/state hypocrisy about sex and calling for their civil rights.

Huge numbers of **Polish** women marched to defend their abortion rights and against the Roman Catholic Church and new Solidarity government in 1989.

In **India**, the women's movement campaigned against dowry murder, **sati**, sexual harassment and rape (especially police rape) with demonstrations and sit-ins **(dharanas)**, agit-prop theatre, songs and exhibitions. They attacked the idea that a raped woman loses her "honour" **(abru)**. Surely it was the male rapist who should be covered with shame? Bihar and Gujerat women, students, housewives and office workers were in the forefront of campaigns against corruption and price rises in the 70s. Tribal women in Maharashtra organized strong protests against male drunkenness and domestic violence. In 1978, a national feminist workshop was set up in Bombay to co-ordinate all the different local groups. **Manushi**, a lively campaigning journal, was set up in Delhi. Feminist classical dancer **Chandraleikha** created a storm when she re-choreographed traditional Indian dance forms to portray the **yoni** as a moving force, strong and active, dancing around the still point of the **lingam**.

In many impoverished and exploited countries in **Asia, Africa** and **South America,** the principal problem confronting the mass of women has been simply getting adequate food and water. The majority of women have a calorie intake below the nutritionally accepted minimum.

In **South Africa**, women have had to confront the deep racial and male/female divisions created by apartheid. In 1956, 20,000 women marched against the government singing:

Now you have tampered with the women
You have struck against rock
You have dislodged a boulder
Now you will be crushed

Feminists have been in the forefront of movements against military dictatorships all round the world.

In **Portugal**, the "Three Marias" stood trial in 1973 for their book exposing the plight of women under the clerico-military regime.

In **Pakistan**, the Women's Action Forum led protests against the military government's Law of Evidence that would make a woman's testimony in a court of law worth only half that of a man's.

In **Iran**, feminists played an active role in the uprisings against the Shah's regime in 1979, and then demonstrated against the anti-women policies of the fundamentalist regime which took its place. 15,000 women seized the Palace of Justice, demanding their rights.

Women in the Arab world have fought for a third way between male-dominated Western values and fundamentalist ones, drawing on women's traditional strengths as traders and poets in Arab society.

In 1982, **Nawal El Saadawi** and other feminists set up a pan-Arab Women's Rights Association based in Cairo. The Feminist Network of Women Living under Muslim Laws compiles dossiers on women's legal rights and their abuses.

The Disappeared and the

From 1976 to 1982, Argentina suffered under a military dictatorship, described as "one of the worse examples of state repression since Hitlerite Germany". In defence of "Western Christian civilization", the regime of Generals set out to cleanse Argentina of all "Communist subversives and trouble-makers" in a systematic campaign of abductions, torture and mass summary executions. It was known as "the Process of National Reconciliation". 20,000 people were jailed without trial, charge or sentence. They were the lucky ones. 30,000 others - men, women and children of all social backgrounds - disappeared without trace.

The majority of the population was silenced by fear of the death-squads. Then, on 30 April 1977, a group of brave women gathered outside Government House in the Plaza de Mayo - May Square.

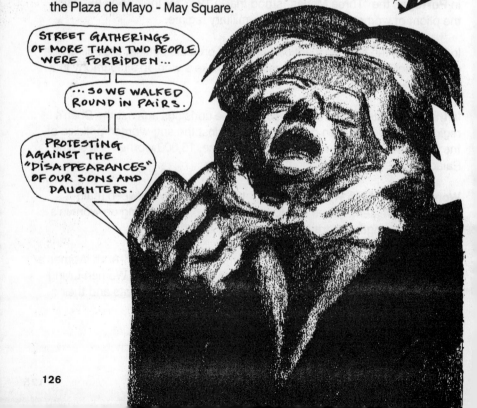

STREET GATHERINGS OF MORE THAN TWO PEOPLE WERE FORBIDDEN...

...SO WE WALKED ROUND IN PAIRS.

PROTESTING AGAINST THE "DISAPPEARANCES" OF OUR SONS AND DAUGHTERS.

Mothers of Plaza de Mayo

The **Mothers of Plaza de Mayo** faced persecution, beatings and death. A group of grandmothers looking for their abducted grandchildren was also formed. The Mother's courage and independent activities as a women-only-group were an outstanding example of "consciousness-raising". Many travelled across the world seeking support, publicizing their cause and establishing links with other women across the globe.

The Mothers inspired many groups of women protesting against human rights violations and brutal military regimes. In 1985, representatives of the Mothers met in London with Iranian women eager to create a similar group in Iran. Iranian and other Latin American women-only groups adopted the Mothers' white kerchief as a symbol of human rights' struggles.

The Greenham Common Peace Movement

In 1980, the Reagan administration advanced a vast new arsenal of nuclear missiles against the Soviet Union. The "Cold War" had gone into storage during the protest years of the Vietnam war. But now, with the opposition at home safely defused, the Pentagon went on the offensive again.

In Britain, feminists seized the leadership of the peace campaign against the new Cruise missiles. They established a Women's Peace Camp outside the US Air Force base at Greenham Common. The **male vs. female** symbolism at Greenham was unmissable.

Armed soldiers INSIDE, defending gigantic phallic symbols of death and destruction.

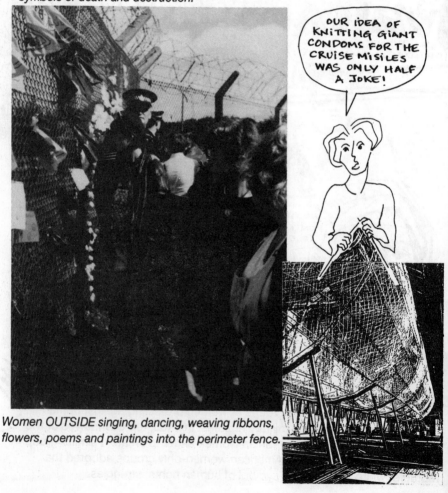

OUR IDEA OF KNITTING GIANT CONDOMS FOR THE CRUISE MISILES WAS ONLY HALF A JOKE!

Women OUTSIDE singing, dancing, weaving ribbons, flowers, poems and paintings into the perimeter fence.

The Greenham Peace Camp gave new impetus to semi-mystical ideas of the "essential" difference between women and men - a protest taken much further by the **Mothers' Manifesto** group in Germany. They argued that women are nurturers, life-givers, the force for peace and love, and men are the aggressors, destroyers, rapists of women and nature.

Take the toys from the boys
Take their hands off the guns
Take their fingers off the trigger
Take the toys from the boys.

Made a bomb out of cotton
Made a bomb out of sugar
Made a bomb out of music
They made a fool out of you.

Take the toys from the boys
Gotta make a living
Take their hands off the guns
Gotta make a killing
Get their fingers off the button
Gotta get promotion
Take the toys from the boys
made a bomb, made a bomb

POISON GIRLS

The Thatcher Years, 1979-90

Ironically, the conservative backlash against feminism began in earnest with the election of the first British woman Prime Minister - Margaret Thatcher.

Thatcher was elected on a programme that was diametrically opposed to everything feminists had been calling for - better health and social services, more rights at work, an open, caring community.

In the US, Ronald Reagan posed as an "economic libertarian", joining with Maggie in a salvationist double-act. The whole idea of community was trashed.

There's no such thing as society. There are individual men and women and there are families. (Feb. 1989)

OH! I LOVE iT WHEN YOU TALK DIRTY!

She's radical enough, but so is gangrene!

The phoney affluence of the 80s - the mindless easy fix of monetarism in Britain and Reaganomics in the US - was a social disaster. All the public services that women depended upon were cut or savagely downgraded. Their limited gains in the trade union movement were wiped out.

What were the effects on women

A new "under-class" of the desperately poor and unemployed was created. In Britain alone, 65% of the "officially" poor are women, many of them single mothers. Women are the fastest growing category of the homeless, nearly half of them fleeing from domestic violence.

Those in work have never been so stressed. In the 1970s, trade unionists campaigned for the 35-hour week. In 1991, the Conservatives still refused to sign the European Social Charter calling for a maximum 48-hour week and a minimum wage.

Social provision has been relentlessly cut back. There is now virtually no free childcare for pre-school children, and the strains of balancing waged work and childcare with poverty, economic dependence and domestic isolation fall largely on women. Cuts in health and education have proportionally more and worse effects on women, because women use the health service more - in pregnancy, childbirth and in caring for sick children. And as the majority of the workforce in schools and hospitals are women, they experience more stress than ever before.

of the Thatcher-Reagan duet?

"The American way of life" has been exported to cities all over the world, with an increase in gangsterism, racial and sexual violence, drug abuse and organized crime. Rape figures have shot up in the last 20 years. In the US, sex-related murders rose by 160% between 1976 and 1984.

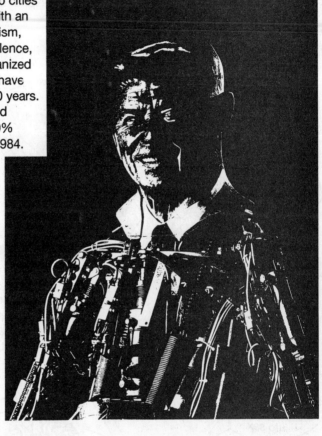

Hope has given way to racial hatred, bigotry and religious fundamentalism. In the US, Christian fundamentalists have been leading an armed crusade against women's fertility rights, firebombing abortion clinics and terrorizing workers and patients. This climate of fear has seriously undermined the **Roe vs Wade** Supreme Court decision. Who are these fundamentalists? Characteristically, young white men from lower income brackets, condemned to "downward mobility" in the Reagan decade, earning less than their fathers, unable to pay ballooning mortgages or put food on the table without their wives' help. Maddened by their lack of economic hope, they took their resentments out on women and ethnic minorities.

Ideas and Issues of the Women's Movement

Women have come a long way since **Mary Wollstonecraft** first set pen to paper. Let's look at some of the aspects of women's lives that the feminist movement has helped to change - and at how far we still have to go!

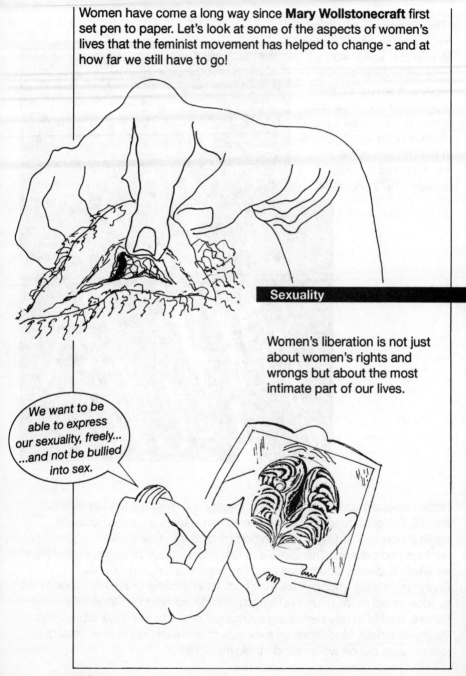

Sexuality

Women's liberation is not just about women's rights and wrongs but about the most intimate part of our lives.

We want to be able to express our sexuality, freely... ...and not be bullied into sex.

The predominant view of sex for centuries has been based around penetration and the male orgasm. Feminists in the 60s drew attention to the joys of the clitoris as well - its myriad network of nerves and veins reaching deep into the pelvis.

The only human organ whose sole function is pleasure. Why has it been ignored?

Feminists have argued for sexual practices free from "the tyranny of the orgasm" - for pleasure that includes the whole personalities of both partners, emotions as well as physical feelings.

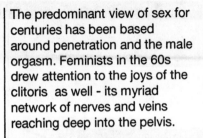

An intimate physical conversation, rather than a time-and-motion study in genital stimulation and climax.

The ART of love-making doesn't have to be reduced to just painting-by-numbers!

Men lose out, too, if they reduce their sexuality to a prick detached from a body that remains ignored, unpleasured and unloved.

But for centuries men have also used sex to punish women.

Women recovering from the trauma of rape need love, support and counselling. Instead they confront a legal system which throws the blame for rape on the victim herself... Under the Islamic Shar'ia Code of Law, a rape victim needs **four** male witnesses to substantiate her testimony. Judges and policemen in the West shortcut the process. **"You're making the whole thing up!"**

The law's definition of rape seems limited to an attack on a complete virgin by a total stranger. This completely denies the reality of late 20th-century sexuality and most women's experience of rape - usually by a boss, work colleague, neighbour, relative or social acquaintance. Judges on rape trials invariably put the victim's whole sex life on trial.

You're unmarried but admit to having had willing sexual relations with other men? One man? Two? How many? And why weren't you willing THIS time?

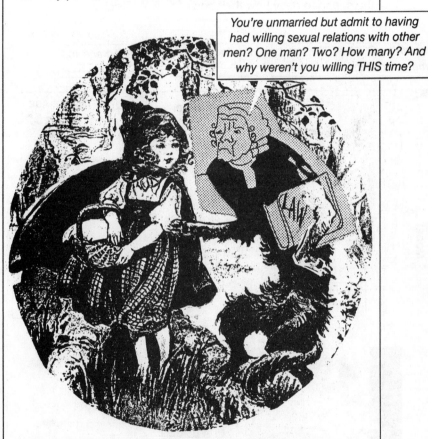

The streets are only safe at night when they are filled with women! The late 70s in Europe saw a whole series of torch-lit "Reclaim the Night" demonstrations by women through violent parts of towns. Many of these night-reclaimers were young women who grew up with feminism as their birthright, a confident new generation of street-wise punks and witches filling the night with their songs of exorcism!

Young women - teenage girls specially - are under enormous pressure to fit in with a perpetual beauty competition - to judge and criticize their own bodies from the OUTSIDE, as men see them, and to deny how their bodies feel, WITHIN.

I wouldn't - COULDN'T - leave home without my make-up on.

I'm too tall for high heels.

Too short and too tall for WHAT?!?

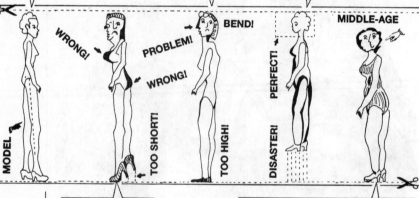

MODEL

WRONG!

WRONG!

PROBLEM!

TOO SHORT!

BEND!

TOO HIGH!

PERFECT!

DISASTER!

MIDDLE-AGE

I'm too short to wear flat shoes.

We're competing against each other for men's approval!

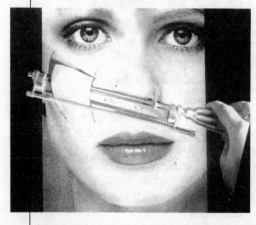

*What shape our arms, legs, bellies, breasts and bottoms **should** be - like speciality cuts in a butcher's shop!*

Many women internalize self-hatred as teenagers. Almost every woman feels there's something "wrong" with some part of her body. Many experience eating disorders. The problem of a deep-down lack of self-esteem is passed on from one unloved, ill-fed mother to her unloved and ill-fed daughter. Feminist therapy groups, women's culture, love and solidarity can be ways to repair the damage and help women love and value themselves again.

We end up in permanent competition with the spectre of the model...

...a tiny minority of girls who devote up to 12 hours a day trying to keep themselves looking flawless.

To which we compare our own, ordinary image in the mirror!

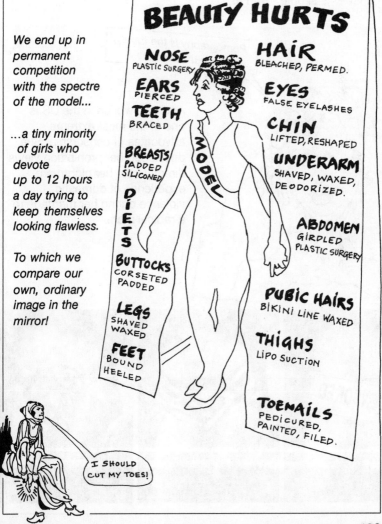

BEAUTY HURTS

NOSE
PLASTIC SURGERY

EARS
PIERCED

TEETH
BRACED

BREASTS
PADDED
SILICONED

DIETS

BUTTOCKS
CORSETED
PADDED

LEGS
SHAVED
WAXED

FEET
BOUND
HEELED

MODEL

HAIR
BLEACHED, PERMED.

EYES
FALSE EYELASHES

CHIN
LIFTED, RESHAPED

UNDERARM
SHAVED, WAXED,
DEODORIZED.

ABDOMEN
GIRDLED
PLASTIC SURGERY

PUBIC HAIRS
BIKINI LINE WAXED

THIGHS
LIPO SUCTION

TOENAILS
PEDICURED,
PAINTED, FILED.

I SHOULD CUT MY TOES!

"The shoe would *not* go on."

Most women have a gut reaction against the images of women's bodies in porn magazines and pin-ups - even if they find some of the images arousing at the same time. It's horrible to see newspaper pictures of our naked bodies blowing down the streets in the rubbish. Why should we let our bodies be used like this? The problem is, how should we deal with it? For some the answer is simple - **Ban it!**

> Pornography is the theory, rape is the practice.

Andrea Dworkin in the US is one of the most extreme advocates of censorship. She developed her prohibition views directly from her nightmare experience of domestic violence during her marriage to a radical man.

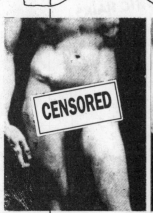

In 1984, Andrea Dworkin and Catherine McKinnon drafted an ordinance to allow women to take civil actions against the production, distribution or sale of pornography on the grounds that its very existence harmed them. The ordinance won massive support from the so-called Moral Majority and other extreme conservative groups. In 1986, the Supreme Court ruled the ordinance unconstitutional in that it violated the First Amendment.

Not only sexual violence but penetrative sexual intercourse is the key moment in women's oppression. All men are rapists, all women are their victims!

But many other feminists disagree with Dworkin's call for censorship. Liberal feminists in the 80s organized anti-censorship lobbies.

Some of us defended Marquis de Sade for his subversive challenge to EVERY taboo.

Susan Sontag

Censoring porn will prove as useless as the Prohibition of alcohol was in the 20s. It will only hand porn over to organized crime.

Angela Carter

Porn is a symptom, not a cause of women's oppression - only part of the wider image that advertises "passive" fashion models, airline hostesses, happy housewives and secretaries. Campaign against THESE degrading images too!

Simone de Beauvoir

Women aren't ALWAYS shown as passive. What about the porn "dominatrix" women armed to the teeth with whips, spurs, knives, etc.?

Why not encourage an ALTERNATIVE pornography which develops a positive pro-woman and lesbian sexuality?

Porn exploits men's anxieties about women and their own inadequacies, expressed as fear and hatred of women. This isn't biological, as Dworkin says, but cultural and open to change.

The unwritten clause at the heart of the marriage vows:

"Do you agree to provide this man with your domestic labour and your sexual and emotional services in exchange for economic support from him as the breadwinner?"

Women's subordinate status in the OUTSIDE world of work, politics and culture...

..and our subordinate position WITHIN the household, family and relationship to a particular man...

These two spheres clearly reflect and reinforce each other!

If you grew up with hopes of equality and a career, it can be traumatic to suddenly find yourself stuck at home with a baby.

Motherhood in our society is praised to the skies - but real-life mothers are ground down by overwork and lack of sleep and get no help at all from society.

Male dominated governments attack single mothers, poor mothers, mothers who cannot cope - yet provide almost nothing in the way of free childcare facilities, child benefits or maternity payments.

For many women, our relationships with our children are among the most precious things in our lives. But how can we be human beings as well as mothers? How can we combine motherhood with citizenship and work?

"Motherhood in our present social state, is the sign and seal, the means and method of a woman's bondage. It forges chains of her own flesh and blood; it weaves chords of her own love and instinct."
(English novelist Mona Caird, 1894)

Whereas fatherhood is quite a different matter!

Sisterhood disappears if women in full-time paid work are made to feel they are not proper mothers. And women raising kids while depending economically on men are made to feel they are not proper human beings. Men can claim to play a far greater role in parenting today, but 90% of all childcare still rests on women's backs, by those in full or part-time work, or by women childminders who have to cope with other people's problems.

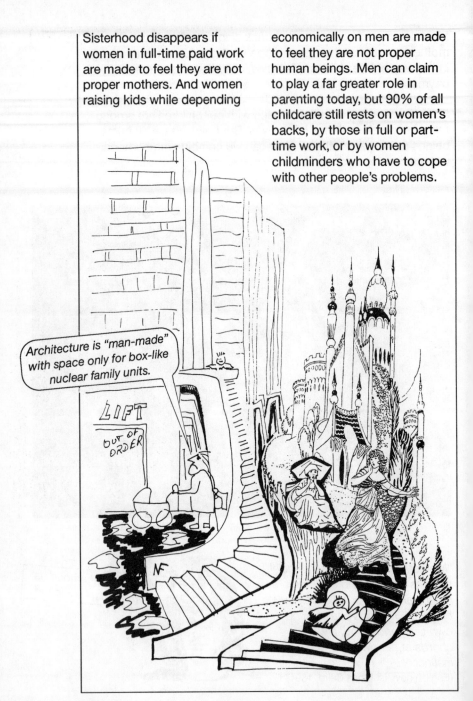

Architecture is "man-made" with space only for box-like nuclear family units.

LIFT

OUT OF ORDER

The question of childcare raises another issue central to feminist consciousness. Are the male and female "natures" we see today completely artificial constructs, as J.S. Mill and other pioneer feminists believed?

Are there any "natural" differences between the sexes - except the ones we are encouraged, educated and bullied into adopting as "male" and "female"?

Here we are at home, says Daddy.

Peter helps Daddy with the car, and Jane helps Mummy get the tea.

Good girl, says Mummy to Jane.

You are a good girl to help me like this.

Good   good   girl

We will never know what the real differences are, until we offer children the widest possible choices to discover what they can BE and can DO - and give them role models of parents with equally free choices!

Ever since the rise of 19th century industrial capitalism, the "nuclear family" has been the male dream of a peaceful shelter from the brutal world of work.

The majority of violent crimes take place within the home. 19th century feminists blamed alcohol as the cause of domestic violence.

Is it really a haven for women and children?

> *Today we say that women's economic dependence on men, which allows men to see us as sub-human, is more central than alcohol or "psychological" problems.*

Feminists in many countries have campaigned to create refuges for battered women and children - safe places where women could begin to rebuild their lives, get advice on rehousing, jobs, schools and money problems.

Battered women from Asian or other ethnic minority communities face even greater problems of language, culture and religion when they try to escape from violent homes.

I don't want my kids to face racism from the whites in a refuge - or racial attacks if I'm rehoused outside my community.

Taking out an injunction against my husband or brother can mean turning them over to police custody or deportation.

MY BROTHERS WILL KILL ME IF I BREAK THE FAMILY **IZZAT** —HONOUR.

And if I am deported, I could face the Muslim death penalty for any relationship I formed since leaving my husband.

Women and children are most at risk from the tyranny of authoritarian men within isolated families - and safest within communities where women's networks are strong.

Men's control over women's fertility - and therefore over their **sexuality** - has long been at the core of women's oppression.

Modern feminists have rescued women's own medical practices of childbirth and fertility-control from a history obscured by male prejudices and self-interest.

There are formulas for abortion in 5,000-year-old Chinese medical texts, in Greek and Roman literature, and in the great Arab treatises on medicine.

Midwives, women-healers and "wise women" were respected figures in so-called "primitive" societies. In medieval Europe, midwives had developed a sophisticated natural pharmacy of herbal remedies.

Contraceptive devices were available. Discs of melted beeswax acted as cervical diaphragms. Sponges soaked in lemon juice were used as spermicides. Condoms made of various materials were in use for thousands of years.

We could prevent or encourage contraception, speed up or ease contractions in childbirth.

An official strategy of persecution against midwives and healers began in the 16th century as European states passed laws especially designed to exclude women from the new "authorized" medical profession dominated by male surgeons.

The **MALLEUS MALEFICARUM**, a witch-hunter's guide of 1486, states that...

"If a woman dare to cure without having studied, she is a witch and must die."

But it's forbidden for us to study!

We weren't allowed in medical schools, universities or research laboratories until the end of the 19th century.

153

And what "progress" did Western medicine make in these centuries of male domination?

Abortion was officially outlawed for the first time in mid-19th century Europe and America.

Gynaecological expertise has been routinely used in the most racist and anti-woman ways to control population. 35% of childbearing Puerto Rican women were sterilized under the auspices of the US Agency for International Development. Between 1973 and 1976 alone, 3,406 Native American women were sterilized in the US.

White genocide didn't stop at Wounded Knee!

Giving birth was no longer something that women **did**, but something that happened **to** them. Male specialists were now in command of the uterus, and the increasing hospitalization of birth led to increasing ignorance.

New techniques and general anaesthetics are routinely applied because these make things more convenient for the doctor.

The medicalized process of childbirth **wants** a woman lying flat on her back, befuddled and terrorized by powerful drugs, and strapped down by a mass of wires, drips and monitors. In short, everything conspires to keep a woman **inactive.**

Stops them bothering me with stupid questions!

Feminists in community health groups, the Active Birth movement and Radical Midwives Association are trying to recover women's rights in childbirth.

Lying flat on your back is the wrong position for childbirth.

The baby's head is pushed down into the perineum, which risks tearing muscles that will need painful stitches.

There are better, more active positions which help to push the baby's head into the right position.

And lying flat produces fear and a sense of helplessness.

You can't use the powerful muscles of your back, belly and abdomen if you're lying flat.

Gravity works FOR the birth, not against it.

Images of naked women are plastered everywhere. But the living **reality** of women's bodies has become taboo - even to ourselves. Women's self-help groups can teach women how to perform our own cervical examinations and pregnancy tests. If we understand our own monthly fertility cycles of ovulation and menstruation, we are in a better position to use our fertility as we choose.

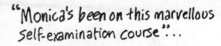

"Monica's been on this marvellous self-examination course"...

Statues of ancient fertility goddesses show a great joy and pride in women's fertility. These figurines give birth standing upright, strong, free and facing forwards into the future. Maybe women today can strive to recapture the strength and pride that these images of our fore-mothers show.

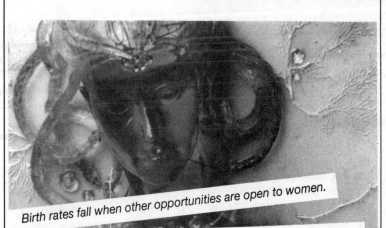

Birth rates fall when other opportunities are open to women.

Birth rates are always highest wherever women are more submerged in domestic life and denied any hope of self-development.

Male experts gave us things like the lethal Dalkon Shield...

And who did the multinational pharmaceutical companies USE to mass-test these products?

The poorest women in Third World countries, who were left without medical aid to cope with the damage done to them!

Big campaigns for a pregnant woman's right to choose for herself whether she needs an abortion or not led to the legalization of abortion in many countries of Europe and North America during the 70s - although it is usually the doctor, not the woman, who has the final right to decide.

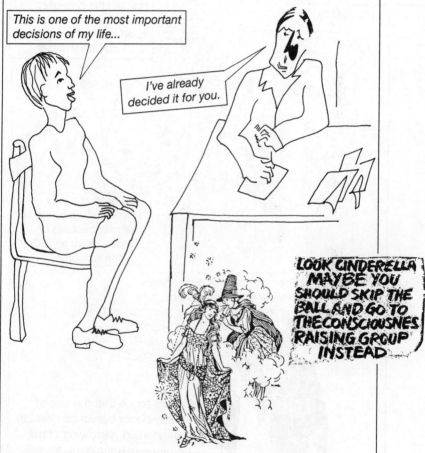

Pregnant women need practical and emotional support - not moralizing - whether they decide they want to terminate a pregnancy or carry on with it. All too often, it is a decision that has to be taken in secret, and its costs borne by the woman.

Feminists are divided over the latest advances in reproductive technology.

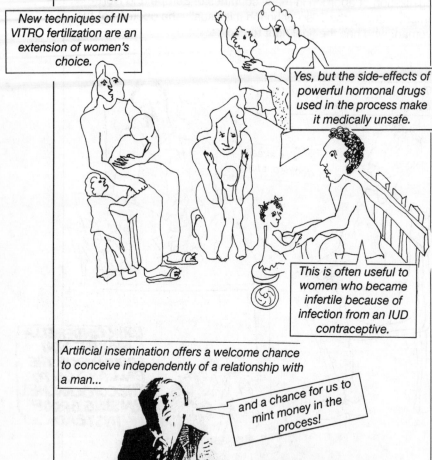

New techniques of IN VITRO fertilization are an extension of women's choice.

Yes, but the side-effects of powerful hormonal drugs used in the process make it medically unsafe.

This is often useful to women who became infertile because of infection from an IUD contraceptive.

Artificial insemination offers a welcome chance to conceive independently of a relationship with a man...

and a chance for us to mint money in the process!

Doctor:

Others argue that the use of sperm-donor banks can lead to a dangerous narrowing of the common genetic pool, as generations of half-brothers and half-sisters grow up unknown to each other.

One of the greatest potential dangers now facing humanity is that of genetic engineering. Identical calves have already been cloned and human cloning is technically possible. The whole process remains shrouded in secrecy because it is considered "socially unacceptable". This hasn't stopped experimentation from going on behind the scenes.

These latter-day Frankensteins threaten every democratic human right. It is in all our interests that control over procreation should be taken away from them - and restored to women, where it belongs.

A proper definition of work must include **all** the labour that needs doing to keep the human race going. That means cooking and cleaning as well as mining and agriculture, wiping babies' bottoms as well as building hospitals. It's all **work**.

The problem is that half these tasks are paid as "proper" work while the other half are unpaid ones that women are **expected** to do at home for free (unless they pay another woman to do them.

For centuries we've been ghettoized into jobs that duplicate our work in the family...
...at HOME, we make the food, do the cleaning, sort out the clothes, do the shopping, care for the children, nurse them when they are ill and look after a man....

...And then we go off to WORK in the food and catering industries, in the clothing trade, as shop assistants....

...we look after the children in schools and play groups, we work in the health service....

...and as secretaries and personal assistants, air hostesses, entertainers, prostitutes and other sex workers...we look after men!

Because most women work in sex-segregated jobs, "equal pay" legislation has been largely ineffective - there are no men doing comparable work for us to be paid equally with!

WOMEN IN AMERICA EARN ONLY 2/3 OF WHAT MEN DO. WOMEN ARTISTS EARN ONLY 1/3 OF WHAT MEN ARTISTS DO.

A PUBLIC SERVICE MESSAGE FROM **GUERRILLA GIRLS** CONSCIENCE OF THE ART WORLD

AN ENGLISHMAN'S HOME IS HIS CASTLE SO LET HIM CLEAN IT.

And what's the result? Women make up half the world's population, perform two-thirds of its work-hours, receive one-tenth of the world's income and own less than one-hundredth of its property.

(UN Report, 1980).

Of course looking after children is important - but isn't it important for men as well as women? **Women will never be able to play a full, balanced role in the economy until men do too - by taking on their full share of childcare and domestic labour!**

This has implications for working hours, too: no one can look after their children properly if they are working 10 hours or more a day.

We want: Shorter working hours! An end to sex segregation at work - and at home!

200 years of feminism have encouraged women to batter down the doors of male domains. A small but significant number of women have battled their way into medicine, law, the universities, and finally politics. There are women carpenters, plumbers and soldiers, women on the floor of stock exchanges, in scientific research, management and the media.

The struggle is a hard one. Women working in male-dominated spheres face resentment and discrimination from men who feel that their work is being downgraded if women are allowed to do it. We face hostile jokes and sexual harassment, with little or none of the support men get from each other - and without a loving wife to nourish and support us and restore our battered egos when we get home tired from the office!

Women in many fields of work have been building up support networks for themselves. Women's groups in trade unions hold informal meetings to share their problems and press for better conditions.

The cut-throat nature of a competitive labour market also means that women workers are set against each other.

...her you choose
use your sexuality
s a weapon, and
re despised for
doing so...

Or you don't use it and are called sexless, uncaring and unnatural.

Worst of all you struggle to climb a few rungs up the promotional ladder, and find that you are not going to rise any further.

...u've reached the "glass-ceiling" - he invisible barrier that no amount of egislation seems to be able to break.

It teaches you that equal opportunity is a myth!

The glass ceiling lets you see where you want to go, but won't allow you to get there.

Feminism has come under many ferocious attacks in its time. After the advances women made in the 1970s, a male "backlash" developed in the USA.

In 1986, a Harvard-Yale survey - now thoroughly discredited - set out to "prove" that all college-educated women over 29 stood less than 20% chance of getting married. The US media went wild about the story. Other "experts" chipped in, claiming that women working full-time were becoming infertile, lonely and unhappy, suffering heart-disease and hair loss, while underneath "craving marriage and security."

The message was clear: equality, feminism and independence make women miserable. A woman's place is in the home, meek, mild and baking cookies. And she'd better get back there - **fast!**

Women stood up to the scam.

The real facts behind the Harvard-Yale survey are that many women are *choosing* to delay marriage - or are simply co-habiting.

Our present-day society *is* stressful for women to live in - but feminism is part of the answer to that, not part of the problem!

And we still have so far to go!

How much have women **really** gained, even in the so-called "advanced" countries? Have we really got everything we fought for in 200 years? Is complete equality won and feminism over? Let's look at Britain which has had a long history of militant feminism.

Haven't women got equal pay?

No. Women in Britain take home 2/3 male pay for the same hours' work (worldwide the figure is 1/10). Most women work in sex-segregated jobs, so "equal pay" legislation cannot help them.

Haven't women got equal opportunities at work?

No. The vast majority of women still work in jobs which are an extension of their traditional "caring, cooking, cleaning" role in the home: the lower echelons of the health and education service, the catering and clothing industries, shop assistants, cleaners. Only 3% of PLC directors in Britain are women and only 4% of judges. 78% of all clerical workers are women, but only 11% are managers.

Haven't women got equal political and civil rights?

No. Only 7% of Members of Parliament are women, only 4% of local authority chiefs and 0.2% of the permanent secretaries in the civil service. Women wanting to stand as parliamentary candidates are grilled about their children and childcare arrangements (or about the reasons for not having children) in a way that men **never** are.

What about free childcare provision, neighbourhood and workplace nurseries and creches?
In Britain, there is virtually no free nursery provision for under-twos, and very little elsewhere in the world.

Free, safe contraception and abortion for any woman who knows she needs it?

Decisions on abortion have been up to (mostly) male doctors ever since abortion was legalized in Britain (and in virtually every other country). Where abortion is illegal, it is in the hands of backstreet abortionists and the police. Current research into contraception receives approximately 0.002% of weapons-research funding.

Freedom to live and love independently from men?

Gutter press attacks on lesbians, and especially on lesbian mothers, are stepping up all the time - despite the fact that children are 94% less likely to be abused in all-female households.

Freedom from rape and domestic violence?

On the contrary, all forms of violence against women have been increasing over recent years, with rising unemployment and growing social tensions.

Further reading...

Feminist classics

Mary Wollstonecraft, *A Vindication of the Rights of Women* (1792). Unique founding statement, full of anecdotes, lively indignation and plain common sense.

John Stuart Mill, *The Subjection of Women*. (1869) A thoroughly decent chap - a model to all his sex - takes up arms in this unanswerable blast against the injustice of one half of the human race being subordinated to the other.

Sylvia Pankhurst, *The Suffragette Movement*. The inside story, full of incidental detail and intrigue. As good as a novel.

Simone de Beauvoir, *The Second Sex*. (1949) Witty, intelligent and scathing, an encyclopaedic account of how women are 'made'.

Sheila Rowbotham, *Woman's Consciousness, Man's World* (1973) Call-to-arms by one of the most influential writers of the women's movement's 'Second Wave'.

The Women's Movement

Anna Coote, Bea Campbell, *Sweet Freedom*. British feminism in the 70s and 80s.

Angela Neustatter, *Hyenas in Petticoats*. The women's movement, now and then.

Robin Morgan, ed., *Sisterhood is Global*. Invaluable directory of women's movements in over 70 countries.

Susan Faludi, *Backlash*. Looks at recent anti-feminist developments.

Women's Identity, Body Politics

Angela Phillips and Jill Rakusen, *Our Bodies, Ourselves*. Classic women's health handbook.

Naomi Wolf, *The Beauty Myth*. Takes the beauty and fashion industry to pieces.

Susie Orbach, *Fat is a Feminist Issue*. Explores women's troubled relationship to food.

Anne Dickson, *A Woman in Your Own Right*. D-I-Y guide to self-assertiveness and self-expression.

Sheila Ernst and Lucy Goodison, *In Our Own Hands*. Introduction to self-help therapy for women.

Juliet Mitchell, *Psychoanalysis and Feminism*. Seminal work, making the connections.

Sexuality

Jane Mills, *Make it Happy, Make it Safe*. Sympathetic guide to sex for young people.

Anne Dickson, *The Mirror Within*. Self-help exploration of female sexuality from a woman's point of view.

Lillian Faderman, *Surpassing the Love of Men*. Historical account spanning 3 centuries of lesbian lives and loving relationships between women.

Susan Brownmiller, *Against Our Will*. Classic analysis of rape and sexual violence.

Varda Burstyn, *Women Against Censorship*. Seminal collection of essays on the pornography debate.

Lynne Segal, Mary McIntosh, *Sex Exposed*. Explores issues of imagery, sexuality and desire.

Motherhood and Families

Ann Oakley, *From Here to Maternity*. Interviews with women about their experiences of pregnancy and childbirth.
Adrienne Rich, *Of Woman Born*. Classic exploration of the contradictions of motherhood.
Ursula Owen, *Fathers and Daughters*. Daughters spill the beans.
Louise Rafkin, *Different Mothers* and *Different Daughters*. Two books of interviews - women talking about having lesbian daughters, children talking about having lesbian mums. Warm, funny, very human.
Elizabeth Wilson, *What is to be Done about Violence against Women?* Down to earth look at the problems - and possible solutions.

Black Studies, Race and Gender

Angela Davis, *Women, Race and Class*. Wide-ranging historical analysis.
bell hooks, *Ain't I a Woman*. Personal and historical account of the devaluation of black women, arguing that the struggles against racism and sexism must be intertwined.
Swasti Mitter, *Common Fate, Common Bond: Women in the Global Economy*. Survey of women's role in the international labour force.
Gita Sahgal, Nira Yuval-Davis, *Refusing Holy Orders*. Pioneering

and passionate feminist response to the new religious fundamentalisms.

Women's culture

The modern women's movement has unleashed a whole renaissance in the field of culture. **Maya Angelou, Lisa Alther, Margaret Atwood, Pat Barker, Toni Cade Bambara, Angela Carter, Anita Desai, Janet Frame, Maxine Hong Kingston, Sara Maitland, Toni Morrison, Suniti Namjoshi, Nawal el Saadawi, Alice Walker** and **Marina Warner** are just a few of the women writers, poets, playwrights, novelists, historians, biographers and science fiction writers - not to mention the visual artists, film-makers, painters, sculptors, cartoonists, photographers and designers, actresses, dancers, performance artists, musicians, singers, song-writers - who have helped to explore previously uncharted territory over the last few decades.

Women's studies

Most colleges now offer women's studies courses, exploring the latest developments in feminist theory. The Open University has brought out a series of books as an introduction to their Women's Studies course - *Imagining Women, Defining Women, Knowing Women, Inventing Women*. Another introduction is *On the Margins: Women's Studies in the 90s*, edited by **J. Aaron** and **S. Walby**. Ring your local college for more details.

Acknowlegements and Credits

Our thanks for their help in our picture research to Rita Keenan and Anne Grennworth at the Women Artists Slide Library, and to Hilary Anderson, Judith Kazantzis and Antonio Santana.

Information Design Workshop and Guy Lane Communications for their technical help.

Steve Griffiths for translating poem on page 7.

Oscar Zarate for his work and support in our last 100 yard dash.

And finally with very special thanks to the following artists and photographers who are an intimate part of this book.
Sylvia Gosse, *"The Printer"*. Page 15.
Frida Kahlo, *"Childbirth"*. Page 19.
Eunice Pinney, *"Two Women"* 1915. Page 28.
Mary Cassatt, *"Mother and Child"*.Page 51.
Marie Constance Charpentier, Page 57.
"Spectable Alley", Whitechapel c.1915, The Streets of East London, Tower Hamlets Public Library. Page 61.
Liubov Popova, *"Painting Relief"* 1916. Page 90.
Ana Godel, *"Drawing"*, Page 97.
Kathe Kollwitz, *"Communal Dormitory"*, *"Woman and Dead Son"* and *"Mothers"*. Pages 95, 89, 96.
Bridget Riley, Page 100.
Oscar Zarate, from *"Lenin for Beginners"* Pages 81, 82, 92.
"The Army in the Factory", Imperial War Museum. Page 79, 96.
Hazel Hirshorn, *"Sojourner Truth"* and *"Woman"*. Pages 35, 99, 131.
Natalia Goncharova. Work in collage. Page 90, 91.

Jacqueline Morreau, *"The Re-Arrest of Emily Pankhurst"*, *"She who weaves"* and *"Hands"*. Pages 75,147,90.
Lynette Molmar & Linda Thornburg,*"Stolen Glances"*, Pandora Books 1991. Page 112
Embroidered picture, Christies, London.From the book The Subversive Stitch :Rozsika Parker, Women's Press Ltd, 1984. Page 116.
Mona Hatoum, from the video, *"So much I want to say"*. Page 123.
Marta Rodríguez, *"Greenham Common"*. Page 128.
Sue Coe, *"Arrest at Greenham Common"* and *"Rape"*. Pages 129, 136.
Poison Girls, Lyrics and Sticker in *"Spray it Loud"*, Pandora 1982. Page 129.
Cath Tate, Photomontages 1, 2 and 3. Pages 130, 131, 132.
Chistine Roche, *"Jeans?"*. Pages 136.
Nina K. Brisley, *"Children's Fairy Tales"*. Pages 137, 139, 145.
Roberta M. Graham, *"From Short Cuts to Sharp Looks"*, in *Women Photographers*, ed. Val Williams, Virago 1986. Page 138.
Judy Chicago, plate from *"The Dinner Party"*. Page 134.
Jo Brocklehurst, *"Boy in Rubber Bondage"* and *"Angie with Marlon"*. Page 142, 143.
Judith Kazantzis, *"Weddings"*. Page 144.
Sutupa Biswas, *"Mother and Child"*. Page 146.
Elena Samperi, *"Happy Families"* and *"Madona"* 1980. Pages 150, 162.
Annie Lawson, *"Self-Examination Course"*. Page 157.
Pacale Petit, *"Mirror"*.Page 158.
Guerrilla Girls, *"One Dollar"*. Page 163.

We Can Do It!

Front Cover: "Rosie the Riveter"

A World War II propaganda poster in the USA to recruit women into vital defence jobs. Women in heavy industry replacing the men drafted into the armed forces increased by 460%. Although 80% of women trained as shipbuilders, riveters and machinists wanted to keep their skilled jobs after the war, they were encouraged to surrender them to returning soldiers, or were laid off or forced back into unskilled work.

Biographical Details

Susan Alice Watkins is a free-lance writer living in London. She joined her first consciousness-raising group in Oxford in 1973 and since then has been involved in abortion campaigns, women's trade union groups, nursery and toddlers' groups and the peace movement.

Marisa Rueda born in Buenos Aires, has lived in London since 1974 working as a community artist dedicated to human rights. Her sculpture has been widely exhibited in women's group and solo exhibitions. Marisa dedicates this book to her daughter Cristina..

Marta Rodríguez born in Buenos Aires, has lived in London since 1974 working as a free-lance designer for the voluntary and community sectors. She has been involved in women's action groups and Latin American human rights and solidarity work, exhibiting in Argentina and travelling twice to Nicaragua.

Country	Votes for women	Equal Rights	Legal Abortion
Argentina	1947	1947	No
Brazil	1932	1962	No
Britain	1918	1975	1967
Canada	1918 (Native peoples, 1960)	1977	1969
China	1949	1952	1955
France	1946	1983	1979
Germany (FDR)	1919	1949	1976
India	1950	1950	1975
Ireland	1922	No	No
Italy	1945	1947	1978
Japan	1945	1947	1948
Nigeria	1977	1979	No
Portugal	1976	1976	No
Russia	1917	1917	1920
USA	1919	No	1973

Index